Acknowledgments

Like all good idea books, this one features the ideas and insights of many. So first and foremost, I'd like to thank all of the homeowners and designers for sharing their personal spaces with us. Thanks, too, to the photographers with the vision to capture these spaces on film.

To those who shared their time, design philosophies, creative ideas, and other resources with me, I owe a special word of appreciation: Juan Arzola of JC Enterprise Services; Bill Feinberg of Allied Kitchen & Bath; Michelle and David Gordon of Desert Sage Builders; Nancy Moore of The Porch Company; and landscape designers Michelle Derviss, Konrad and Denise Gauder, Jim Harrington, Richard McPherson, Jackye Meinecke, Warren Simmonds, Michael Thilgen, David Thorne, and Jeni Webber. Thanks to Trudy Cooper for her assistance and support, as well as to the team of editors, designers, and others at Taunton Books, including Carolyn Mandarano, Stefanie Ramp, Jenny Peters, and Wendi Mijal. My gardening hat goes off to all of you.

Contents

Introduction

Dorothy first uttered the words, "There's no place like home," more than 60 years ago in the classic film *The Wizard of Oz*. Those same words have become a mantra for the early 21st century. We spend our days in office meetings, carpooling, and commuting on overcrowded interstates. Is it any wonder that we relish the familiarity and comfort of home at the end of the day?

One of the hottest trends in home design is the creation of outdoor rooms—all the comfort of the family room, kitchen, and dining room in an alfresco setting. Interior designers are now applying their skills to exterior spaces, while landscape designers now have a much broader palette of materials and furnishings from which to choose. Manufacturers have responded by introducing more comfortable and decorative furnishings, outdoor hearths, and lighting fixtures that add ambience to any gathering, as well as a broader range of equipment for cooking meals outside—whether it's an inexpensive portable grill or a top-of-the-line outdoor kitchen with all the bells and whistles.

Kids of all ages are benefiting from this mounting enthusiasm for outdoor living. Play structures can be customized with modular features to accommodate the interests of growing children. Manufacturers have introduced game courts for backyard recreation that are easier on the

joints than concrete or asphalt. And new technology in swimming pool design has resulted in a broader range of pool styles and features that are easier to install than ever before. Even synthetic putting greens have made their way into the backyard.

In the end, it's all about relaxing—taking a break from the stresses of day-to-day living. Whether that means cooking a gourmet dinner for friends, relaxing in the spa, gathering around the fireplace with family, retreating to a backyard studio, or playing bocce ball with your neighbors, you can design an outdoor living area that makes the most of your property and makes it fun to spend time at home, outdoors.

TO LIFE BOATS.

Cooking and Dining

FAMILY AND FRIENDS HAVE GATHERED IN THE KITCHEN FOR YEARS—not just to eat but also to catch up on the day's activities and socialize. With the growing interest in casual outdoor entertaining, it's natural for such gatherings to shift to backyard cooking areas.

Enhanced grill features, innovative entertainment islands, and self-sufficient outdoor kitchens have made cooking and dining alfresco easier than ever before, whether it's tossing a few burgers on the grill or creating a gourmet meal from scratch. Although you can get by with a portable grill for basic backyard barbecues, investing in a permanent outdoor cooking center can simplify food preparation and serving, while also accommodating more elaborate affairs. These units can include multiple cooking surfaces, extended counter space, under-counter refrigerators, and bar sinks, all of which make outdoor dining (and cleanup) easier and more enjoyable.

Equally important as cooking areas are eating areas. Comfortable, stylish furnishings have made it a pleasure to relax and dine in the sun or beneath a starry sky. From chic bistro tables to grilling islands with bar seating to classic teak dining sets with expandable seating, weather-resistant furniture is available to suit nearly every decorating style and gathering size.

◀ CONVENIENTLY LOCATED just beyond the kitchen door, this dining nook offers a comfortable place to gather for meals that have been prepared in the kitchen or on the grill. The low hedge, cut-stone paving, and vine-covered arbor create the sense of an outdoor room.

▲ WEATHER CONDITIONS are always a consideration when planning an outdoor cooking and dining area. The tall hedge and house wall screen this grill from breezes, and the umbrella can be raised or lowered throughout the season depending on the sun's intensity.

▶ PLACING THIS GRILL along the outer edge of the patio helps define the space and frees up the patio itself for dining, entertaining, or other activities. It also keeps the heat away from activity areas.

Choosing a Location

COOKING AND DINING AREAS created on decks, patios, porticos, or porches offer convenience to kitchens and baths and make it easy to access gas, water, and power for grills or cooking centers. Their proximity to the house also tends to encourage frequent use.

However, cooking and dining areas located away from the house can offer a greater sense of outdoor living and may capitalize on special views or serve as gathering places around pools or gardens. Because they are located farther from the house, these areas should be designed with greater self-sufficiency in mind. Additional amenities and storage may need to be installed or constructed, and professionals may need to be hired for involved projects, like wiring.

▲ TWO SEPARATE DINING AREAS make this space adaptable. Counter seating, under the pergola, is convenient for snacks, conversing with the chef, and quick weeknight dinners. The dining area nearby is preferred for more leisurely sit-down dinners and larger gatherings with friends.

▲ THIS OUTDOOR KITCHEN is protected from the elements by a portico but requires a grill hood to vent away smoke. The kitchen also features a prep sink, under-counter refrigerator, and storage cabinets. Tile countertops and a tile backsplash give the kitchen character.

▶ THE PATTERNED FLOOR AND BEAMED CEILING define this outdoor dining room, situated just steps away from the sheltered outdoor kitchen and hearth. The cabinet above the hearth houses a television, making this seating area a favorite gathering spot on game night.

◄ THIS INNOVATIVE DINING AND FOOD PREPARATION AREA was created with inexpensive materials. The snack bar was built from recycled roofing metal and an old sink while the chairs were rescued from a flea market. The table and countertops display tile mosaics laid in concrete by the homeowner.

Bringing in the Pros

CONSTRUCTING AN OUTDOOR KITCHEN can be a lot like building or remodeling an indoor kitchen. Chances are you'll need access to water, power, and gas lines. If you're installing a grill, the housing unit and adjacent cabinetry must meet fire-safety standards. And all sinks, refrigerators, and ice makers require adequate waste-water drainage.

The more complex the project, the more a design professional can help simplify the process. A kitchen designer, landscape architect, or general contractor can help you make the most of available space, sort out design options, plan for utilities, locate construction materials, acquire any appropriate building permits, and oversee installation.

▲ POSITIONED ALONG THE EDGE of the backyard to take advantage of a view of California's Simi Valley, this outdoor kitchen is an inviting backyard destination. An open railing behind the kitchen retains views while ensuring safety on the steep site.

Grills

Food simply tastes better when it's cooked outdoors. Whether it's the fresh air, searing coals, or relaxed atmosphere that makes the difference, grilling ranks among today's hottest outdoor activities. In response to this growing market, manufacturers have introduced grills in every price range and with an expanded array of features, such as multiple fuel options, assorted configurations, and innovative new accessories.

Homeowners can choose from portable, pedestal, cabinet, drop-in, or site-built grills and fire them up with wood, charcoal, propane, natural gas, electricity, or infrared heat. These grills can be customized to suit cooking preferences with adjustable fire pans, side burners, smoker boxes, rotisseries, woks, warming ovens, deep fryers, griddles, and searing grids. This array of high-tech options, along with built-in temperature gauges, long-handled utensils, grilling baskets, specialty cookbooks, and, of course, just the right apron, can turn novice and experienced cooks into grilling enthusiasts in no time.

▼ MULTIPLE GRILLING RACKS on this site-built charcoal barbecue allow foods to be cooked over hot or warm coals. A nearby egg-shaped kamado cooker is used for smoking meats. Charcoal, a charcoal-chimney starter, and grilling supplies are stored in a cabinet beneath the granite countertop.

◄ TASK LIGHTING is an important addition near grills where ambient light falls off sharply after dark. Here, a lamp was mounted in the stucco-and-tile wall above the grill. A second task lamp was added near the corner sink.

▲ THE STAINLESS-STEEL CABINET DOORS beneath this grill provide access to the inner workings of the natural-gas grill. (On a propane grill, the tanks would be located here.) This space is also used for storing tools such as a grill thermometer and wire brush.

► THIS PROFESSIONAL-GRADE, stainless-steel, eight-burner gas grill was designed to feed a crowd. Ample Btu and a large cooking surface make it easy to keep up with the demands of a large gathering. The butcher-block island on casters can be moved about as needed.

▼ THIS MEDIUM-SIZED GAS GRILL is perfect for family dinners and features an additional burner useful for preparing side dishes. Gas grills are a smart choice for those who grill on weeknights because they heat up quickly and require minimal attention.

▲ SMOKER BOXES are now available on many gas grills. Wood chips, such as mesquite, apple, or hickory, are soaked in water and placed in the smoker boxes (or in foil packets placed on the grate). The steaming chips flavor the meat during a slow-cooking process.

Smart Shopping

IT'S EASY TO GET SIDETRACKED by all the bells and whistles when shopping for a grill. The most important things to consider are how large a grilling surface you need and what type of fuel you prefer. Carry along a list of desired features and know how you will use your grill: nightly or just occasionally, for small gatherings or large parties, year-round or just in the summer. Also, look for these features:

- Sturdy construction
- Built-in thermometer—not essential, but convenient
- Rust-proof grill racks
- Easy-to-remove ash or drip pans
- At least two heat zones on a gas grill
- Adjustable vents on the top and bottom of charcoal grills

GRILL STYLES

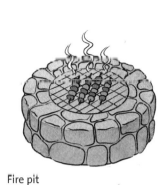

Fire pit

Freestanding portable

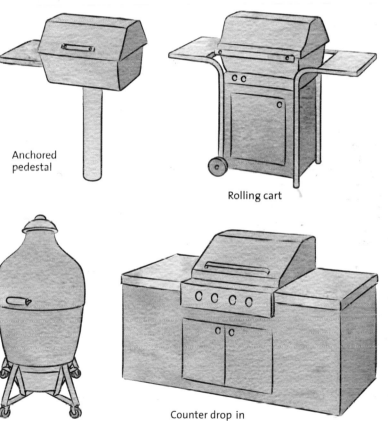

Anchored pedestal

Rolling cart

Kamado cooker

Counter drop in

▲ ROTISSERIE ATTACHMENTS FOR GRILLS can be used for roasting whole birds or large cuts of meat. They rotate for slow, even cooking. Some gas grills feature an infrared rotisserie burner, which provides very hot, concentrated heat to speed the cooking process.

▶ JUST ABOUT ANYTHING that can be cooked in a conventional oven can be cooked in a wood-fired oven, but pizzas and breads are the most popular. This clay, wood-burning oven was hand-crafted by the owners, who were inspired by Asian design. Prefabricated ovens and professionally built ovens are also available.

A Simple Barbecue Pit

OLD-FASHIONED BARBECUE PITS, **like those still found in many campgrounds, offer an easy, affordable, and nostalgic method of backyard grilling over wood or coals. They can be built with concrete blocks, bricks, or stone, with stationary or adjustable grill racks. The building materials for these grills may be dry-stacked for temporary use or mortared for greater permanence. As an alternative to a grill rack, it is also possible to grill over a fire using wire baskets, long-handled skewers, or a mesh screen laid over the firebox. Just be sure to use hot pads so you don't get burned, and keep a safe distance from any flames.**

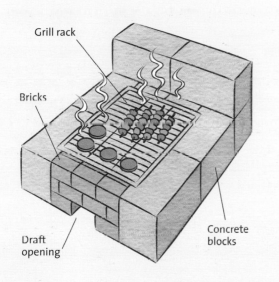

Grill rack

Bricks

Draft opening

Concrete blocks

▶ THIS KAMADO-STYLE COOKER, which was designed to burn hardwood charcoal, can be used for either grilling or smoking. Its compact size is more appropriate for small gatherings and makes it ideal for tight spaces such as this condominium courtyard.

◀ ONE OR MORE SIDE BURNERS, which can be used with or without the grill, are handy for simmering sauces, boiling corn or lobster, sautéing vegetables, or steaming side dishes. They can also keep meats warm as they come off the grill.

▲ THE SMALL SECTION OF THIS CHARCOAL GRILL is used when cooking just for two, while both sections can be fired up when serving a crowd. An all-day fire can also be maintained in the small unit, allowing meats to be smoked slowly in the larger section.

Cooking Centers

COOKING CENTERS ARE THE NEXT STEP beyond the grill itself. They may be simple cabinets built around drop-in charcoal or gas grills for food preparation and serving, or fully equipped outdoor kitchens with generous counters, storage cabinets, prep sinks, under-counter refrigerators, ice makers, and other outdoor-grade appliances.

On a smaller scale, a bar or entertainment island is an affordable and practical accompaniment to a freestanding grill. Many of these units come with wheels so that they can be easily repositioned depending on the occasion. In many instances, cabinets with countertops can be built around existing grills. When choosing materials, keep in mind the cooking area's location. Beneath the cover of a porch or portico, outdoor kitchens can feature interior-grade materials, but if exposed to the elements, they should be constructed with durable, all-weather materials.

▼ A REFRIGERATOR makes this grilling station more functional. In addition to storing cold drinks, it's a convenient place to stash afternoon snacks and sandwich ingredients. Extra meat can be kept cool until tossed on the grill, and salads can be kept fresh until serving time.

◄ BY ADDING SEVERAL SHORT COUNTER-
TOPS near the bar sink, the homeowners can separate food and beverage
preparation from the serving area. The
broad, curving counter can be used for
serving a meal buffet style or adapted
for dining with the addition of stools.

Battle of the BTU

SINCE BRITISH THERMAL UNITS (BTU) vary from
one grill to another and are often hyped
in sales literature to make a grill sound more
powerful, it's natural to think that more is
better. Although Btu reflect the heat output
of the burners, they are more closely related to
fuel consumption than to how hot a grill gets;
this is due to the fact that grill size, construction materials, and overall design also affect
the heat level. As a rule of thumb, plan on 100
Btu per sq. in. of grill space. A 300-sq.-in. grill
needs approximately 30,000 Btu to operate
efficiently. Higher Btu may simply waste fuel
or be a sign of inefficient design.

► THIS SMALL PREP SINK, sheltered
beneath a portico, is ideal for scrubbing
vegetables and washing hands. It is
also convenient for rinsing dirty dishes
before carrying them to the kitchen. In
a pinch, the sink can be filled with ice
to chill canned drinks.

◄ NONFLAMMABLE, WATER-RESISTANT MATERIALS, such as the stone and stucco used here, are preferable for outdoor cabinets. Concrete block with brick or tile veneer is also an excellent choice. Provided a metal fire shield is constructed around the grill, rot-resistant wood cabinets may be used as well.

► THIS COOKING CENTER makes the most of minimal space. The raised counter extension allows for both grilling and pull-up seating on a single cabinet base. And building the posts into the counter was also a space-saving adaptation.

Anatomy of an Outdoor Kitchen

AN OUTDOOR KITCHEN CONTAINS many, but not usually all, of the same elements as an indoor kitchen. Dishwashers, for instance, are not as common outdoors because dishes are often washed and stored inside the house for sanitary reasons. Also, omitting the dishwasher eliminates the need to run hot-water lines to the outdoor kitchen.

Sinks, adequate lighting, and ample counter space rate high both indoors and out. At least some storage space is generally considered essential outdoors, especially if the kitchen is located a long way from the house. Refrigerators and ice makers, while not essential, are popular outdoor appliances that make entertaining easier.

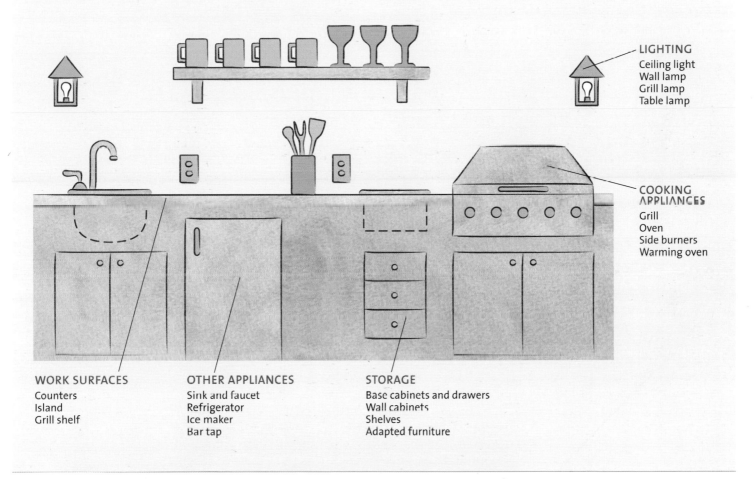

LIGHTING
Ceiling light
Wall lamp
Grill lamp
Table lamp

COOKING APPLIANCES
Grill
Oven
Side burners
Warming oven

WORK SURFACES
Counters
Island
Grill shelf

OTHER APPLIANCES
Sink and faucet
Refrigerator
Ice maker
Bar tap

STORAGE
Base cabinets and drawers
Wall cabinets
Shelves
Adapted furniture

◄ FUNCTIONALITY IS A HALLMARK of this triangular work space, which occupies one corner of a square patio. It features several expanses of tile countertops for food preparation and serving, as well as plenty of under-counter bays for a trash receptacle, recyclables, and storage.

► A KITCHEN COUNTER WITH A SINK and under-counter refrigerator was built on the back of this stairwell that leads from an upper deck. As a space-saving convenience, a portable grill is kept in the closet, where it can be rolled out when needed.

▼ THESE HOMEOWNERS ALREADY HAD A PORTABLE GRILL, so they simply built a cabinet with generous counters and storage space around it. When the time comes, they can lift the grill out of the opening and drop in a new one.

Counter Configurations

THERE ARE AT LEAST AS MANY counter configurations for outdoor kitchens as there are for indoor kitchens. One cook may want to do little more than grill meat. Another may want to have all the amenities of an indoor kitchen, plus a wood-burning pizza oven. Some prefer areas dedicated solely to cooking, while others use counters for food preparation, cooking, eating, and entertaining.

A traditional work triangle created with a sink, grill, and refrigerator is as efficient outdoors as it is indoors, but it's not essential. The key is designing something that suits a particular style of cooking and entertaining. There are many options, including single counters and galley arrangements, as well as curved, triangular, L-shaped, and U-shaped configurations.

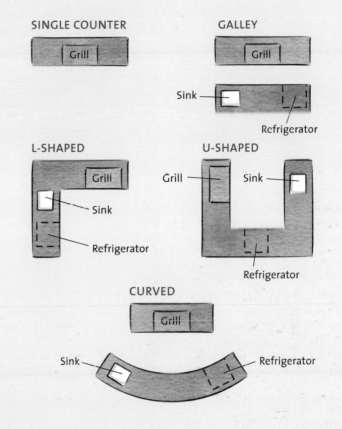

► THE FAUCET ON THIS OLD CERAMIC SINK is hooked up to waterlines in the adjacent building. By placing an outdoor sink near a building, construction costs can be kept to a minimum because existing utility lines can be tapped into easily.

▲ THIS PREFABRICATED GRILL CABINET features a countertop that extends in a circular fashion on one end to accommodate pull-up seating for two beneath a built-in shade umbrella. It sits on a stucco and faux-stone-veneer cabinet base.

▶ THIS GRILL, REFRIGERATOR, AND FOOD PREPARATION AREA was recessed into an exterior wall. The owners chose to match the veneer of the hood vent to the surroundings so that a fireplace on an adjacent wall would remain the primary focal point of the pavilion.

Choosing a Countertop

WHEN CHOOSING OUTDOOR COUNTERTOPS, durability is as important as good looks. The most durable and elegant choices include granite and marble, which are stain resistant, water resistant, and cool to the touch even in direct sunlight. Glazed tile, while not quite as durable or natural looking as granite or marble, offers many of the same benefits at a fraction of the cost and with far greater variety in color, pattern, and texture.

Many additional materials can be used outdoors but require more care or careful use. Artificial stone countertops are often a good option, but their ability to withstand the weather may vary, so check with the manufacturer before placing an order. Unglazed tiles, as well as bluestone, flagstone, and slate, can be beautiful and rugged—provided they are sealed for stain resistance, easier cleaning, and to help prevent the spread of germs. Stainless steel is a possibility for shaded areas, but it will heat up quickly if placed in direct sunlight; it can also scratch. And when exposed to salt spray from the ocean, stainless steel has a tendency to rust.

Laminate countertops should be avoided outdoors, as they will quickly deteriorate when exposed to sun, rain, and freezing temperatures. Wood should also be avoided; it is flammable, does not weather the elements well, and is hard to keep sanitary in outdoor conditions.

▲ THE POLISHED GRANITE COUNTERTOP on this stainless-steel cabinet withstands an outdoor setting well. It is easy to clean, provides a smooth working surface, is heat and stain resistant, and is durable even in cold climates because it is porous and thus won't crack when frozen.

◄ THIS OUTDOOR KITCHEN is used primarily for grilling and additional storage. The traditional indoor cabinetry matches the cabinets in the adjacent kitchen (viewed through the windows). The portico provides plenty of shelter to protect the wood finishes, and the entire area has been screened in.

Alfresco Dining

Whether cooking indoors or out, it's refreshing to dine alfresco. On cool days, a sunny spot is ideal. In hot weather, something shaded may be more suitable. A market umbrella or retractable awning can be opened or closed as conditions change, and a vine-covered arbor provides increased shade as the season warms up.

Before purchasing furniture, give some thought to how it will be used. A bistro table may be ideal for a light lunch or romantic dinner for two, but it won't accommodate a growing family for dinner. A dining table with optional leaves can be easily adjusted if gatherings vary in size, and a buffet-style serving area is an excellent option when entertaining a crowd. And for space-saving convenience, a cooking island can double as a bar with stools. Also consider the style and materials of furnishings, as they vary in weight, durability, and ease of care.

▶ THIS COZY PATIO IS JUST THE RIGHT SIZE for a small family or two couples to share a sunset dinner. Although it is open to views and a ceiling of sky, the low wall helps define the space and create a sense of enclosure.

▼ THE TALL BACKS AND SIMPLE LINES on these teak chairs add visual weight and create an atmosphere of understated elegance on this low deck, where the view is clearly the main attraction. High-backed chairs provide better support and greater comfort when sitting for long periods.

▶ DINING AREAS DESIGNED AS DESTINA-TIONS, like this nook in a sandy dune, can turn dinner into an outdoor adventure. The key to success is advanced planning—the lighter the load and the fewer trips made back and forth to the house, the better.

◀ TEAK IS THE MOST WIDELY ADAPTABLE of all outdoor furniture materials. It is sturdy and rot resistant, and it weathers beautifully to a tawny gray. It is equally at home in a formal landscape or in a more relaxed setting, as illustrated here.

▲ WITH A LITTLE IMAGINATION, dining outdoors can make you feel years younger. This casual setting—a cozy space enclosed by lush foliage and a soft carpet of mulch—calls to mind secret gardens and childhood tea parties.

◄ THE FURNITURE, DINNERWARE, GARDEN STRUCTURES, containers, and plantings work in unison to carry out a sophisticated Asian style and lush green color scheme in this outdoor dining room. Food and soothing music from the outdoor sound system will add the finishing touches for a dinner party.

Creating a Cozy Space

THE MOST INVITING DINING AREAS are cozy and convey a sense of intimacy. On urban lots, that can often be achieved by providing screening between houses. Trees and mixed plantings make an effective natural buffer, while strategically placed wood fences or masonry walls can screen unwanted views and create a sense of enclosure. If neighboring houses are two-story structures, consider adding an arbor over the dining area for additional screening.

On large or open lots, it may be more effective to enclose only the dining area, leaving glimpses of the yard or garden beyond while still creating a roomlike atmosphere. Walls and fences can be covered with vines, espaliered trees, wall planters, fountains, mirrors, and other decorative objects to create a space with personality. Likewise, on a large deck or patio, a cluster of planted containers can help define a smaller, cozier area specifically for dining.

▲ EVEN THOUGH THIS FOUR-PERSON TABLE sits out in the lawn, a cozy dining area has been created by constructing a tall, wooden privacy fence and by planting a dense screen of shrubs, ornamental grasses, and flowering perennials.

► THIS FESTIVE TIKI HUT is the hub of backyard activities. Located in southern Florida, where it is blistering hot much of the year, the shade and ceiling fan are much appreciated. The bar is a casual gathering spot as well as a place to dine.

▲ ALTHOUGH IT IS A CONTINUATION of the broader deck, this dining area is clearly defined by its placement on a lower level. The different levels help to visually connect the house with the landscape, making the gathering area a central point of focus.

◄ THIS HOMEOWNER MADE HIS OWN DINING TABLE from objects one might expect to find around the garden—an oversized ceramic planter and a round-cut stone. Such elements help the seating area look comfortably at home against the backdrop of a soothing foliage garden.

◄ A RUGLIKE PATTERN of stone paving beneath this iron-and-glass dinner set creates a colorful, roomlike atmosphere. Similar effects can be achieved with brick patterns, stone and tile mosaics, and decorative concrete stains.

▼ THIS PICNIC TABLE is advantageously positioned between the lawn and a lush garden to create a cozy setting. The paving defines the patio, and container plantings are strategically positioned to clearly mark the passageways between the spaces.

◀ THIS OUTDOOR ROOM PROVIDES a casual eating area, making use of versatile, space-saving side tables rather than one large dining table. The space is clearly defined by the arbor, boulder garden, and broadened area laid in mortared stone.

▼ THESE HOMEOWNERS BUILT A DECK to make the most of their steep lot, and in doing so, they created a magical dining area that is, literally, in the treetops. The blue paint and accent items reinforce the impression of being near the sky.

▲ EVEN WHEN SPACE IS TIGHT, as it is on this deck, it is important to provide passages 3 ft. to 4 ft. wide for traffic flow. As a rule of thumb, allow at least 8 ft. square for a table that seats four.

Recycled Ideas

RECYCLED BUILDING MATERIALS look right at home outdoors, and using them reduces the amount of waste sent to landfills. Special finds from the local salvage yard or flea market can also give instant personality and character to an outdoor room. Consider these possibilities:

- Old bricks give patio floors a lived-in look.
- Worn-out chandeliers easily convert for candlelight.
- Pots and jars shine as candleholders or flower vases.
- Old sinks enhance an outdoor kitchen.
- Broken dishes and tiles enliven countertops when laid in mosaic patterns.
- Old signs are eye-catching mounted on entertainment islands.
- Metal pails filled with ice are perfect for serving chilled drinks at parties.

▲ EATING IN THE GARDEN is a celebration of where food comes from. This shaded dining table is surrounded by a series of raised-bed gardens featuring vegetables, herbs, and flowers. The crushed gravel creates a casual patio setting and drains quickly after a rain.

▲ CANDLELIGHT TRANSFORMS THIS TROPICAL GARDEN SETTING into a romantic one once the sun goes down. In addition to candleholders on the table, lanterns with candles have been hung on low posts around the perimeter of the stone patio for ambience as well as safety.

◄ THIS COOKING AND DINING AREA is located beneath a vine-covered arbor, anchored by bold columns that match those on the house. It is a large area conducive to entertaining and doubles as a passageway to the swimming pool and putting green below.

Mosquito Control

With the increased spread of mosquito-borne viruses, bug control is a growing concern for many homeowners. The best defense against mosquitoes is eliminating any standing water where they might breed. In ponds, add moving water or introduce fish to eat the larvae; mosquito tablets may also help.

Spray yourself with bug repellent, especially if you're exposed to mosquitoes for a prolonged period. And if that isn't enough, place a container of geranium oil repellent on a table, or spread an organic powder repellent on your lawn. Mechanical options for control include fuel-powered mosquito traps that attract and catch blood-seeking insects such as mosquitoes, no-see-ums, and sand gnats.

▲ EVEN CITY DWELLERS can have a private outdoor dining retreat. What might have been wasted space beneath a staircase is cleverly utilized to create a cozy, shaded dining spot for two. It is surrounded and softened by lush greenery and brightened by colorfully painted columns.

▲ THE WOODEN ARBOR DEFINES the ceiling and corners of this outdoor room, which is used for both grilling and eating. The grill is located in the far corner, away from the eating counter, to minimize the effect of the heat and smoke it generates.

Entertaining Outdoors

FOR CAUSAL GET-TOGETHERS, ENTERTAINING OUTDOORS IS THE WAY TO GO. Fresh air and warm sunshine immediately put guests at ease, while a starlit ceiling and flickering candlelight offer drama and romance in the evening. Everyone loves spending time outdoors, and spaces can be adapted for entertaining all age groups.

Patios, porches, and decks that span the space between the house and yard offer the convenience of indoor amenities along with the relaxed atmosphere of the great outdoors. And gathering spaces that flow seamlessly from a home's interior to exterior can create a continuous living area. Small patios and porches are ideal for intimate gatherings, while broad terraces or decks better handle a crowd. Several gathering areas can suit different occasions or permit crowds to break up into smaller conversation groups. Regardless of the space, walls, fences, hedges, and arbors can establish a roomlike atmosphere conducive to entertaining, especially in densely populated urban neighborhoods.

For laid-back get-togethers, comfortable seating is a must—whether it's chaise lounges placed on a sunny terrace, cushioned sofas and occasional chairs clustered in a conversation group, or sturdy chairs pulled up around a table. And freestanding or retaining walls built at sitting height help define a space while also providing additional seating when a party is at overflow capacity.

◄ THIS COZY PATIO, which has been carved out of a wooded hillside, is located farther away from the back door than most patios, but the shady oak canopy and view make it a compelling gathering spot for friends and family.

Patios and Terraces

MOST PROPERTIES HAVE SPACE for at least one patio or terrace. It could be a dining patio near the kitchen, a broad terrace beyond the living room, an intimate patio just outside the bedroom, or a viewing terrace in the garden. Whereas patios are built on flat ground, terraces are carved out of a slope, which means that they often have retaining walls or are accessed by steps. Patios may have walls, too, but they will be freestanding walls built for seating, privacy, or a sense of enclosure.

Patios and terraces can be enhanced with creative paving materials, softened with plantings, and made more inviting with furniture and decorative accessories. They may include areas for cooking and dining or be geared strictly toward casual conversation. In most climates, covering at least part of a patio or terrace with shade from a tree or structure will make it more welcoming.

◄ THIS SUNKEN TERRACE is large enough to accommodate two large dining tables with room to spare, yet it exudes a cozy atmosphere because it is surrounded by the house, retaining walls, and a wisteria-draped arbor that extends over half of the space.

▲ BECAUSE WHITE AND RED ARE SUCH DOMINATING COLORS in a landscape, they must be used cautiously. They are used to good effect on this casual patio, capturing both attention and the imagination—perhaps even compelling guests to shell a few peas over drinks and conversation.

◄ THIS BACKYARD IS NO MORE THAN 12 FT. DEEP, but dense plantings give it a sense of privacy, making it comfortable for entertaining. The flagstone pavers are dry-laid and planted with creeping herbs, which allows rainfall to soak easily into the ground.

▲ THESE DUAL PATIOS serve different roles. The upper patio acts as a transitional space between the house and surrounding landscape, making it ideal for indoor-outdoor entertaining. The lower patio, which overlooks a lake, is preferred for casual dinners and sunset cocktails with close friends.

◀ BY LAYING LOCAL FLAGSTONE and surrounding it with boulders and ferns, this patio makes an immediate connection with the natural landscape. The naturalistic-style plantings and extensive use of foliage plants (rather than brightly colored flowers) help establish a soothing setting for casual, intimate get-togethers.

Festive Tents for Any Season

TENTS ARE AN EASY AND AFFORDABLE WAY to add a festive note to any backyard gathering. They come in bright or neutral colors, as well as several styles, and range in size from 8 ft. by 8 ft. to more than 30 ft. by 50 ft. If wind, rain, or cold temperatures are an issue, most have side curtains that can be dropped and, with proper ventilation, portable heaters can be used in flame-retardant tents to warm up the space even in winter.

For frequent use or permanent placement in a backyard, reasonably priced tents are available for purchase, but for large tents or infrequent affairs, renting is a practical alternative.

▼ THIS BROAD PATIO serves many functions. One person can nap in a hammock, several people can chat comfortably while sitting in chairs or on stools, a group can gather around the table, and furniture can be easily shifted to host a party.

► WHEN HOSTING LARGE GATHERINGS, guests appreciate a small, quiet place in which to escape for a more personal conversation with a few friends. This sunken stone patio is perfect for that. Guests can lean against the wall, sit on the steps, or share the chaise.

▼ CREATIVE PAVING CAN MAKE even the smallest spaces special and serve as a conversation starter. In addition to the unique spiral mosaic and inset terra-cotta-colored tiles, the planting pockets filled with colorful flowers along the edge of the patio add a festive, whimsical air.

◄ THIS PATIO WAS DESIGNED specifically with the lake view in mind. The subtlety of the clean lines, natural construction materials, and simple furnishings allow the view to dominate, while giving the homeowners and friends a place to gather at the water's edge.

Walls Increase Seating Capacity

LOW RETAINING WALLS AND FREESTANDING WALLS can do double duty. Not only can they define a patio or hold back earth on a sloped terrace, but they can also provide casual seating that easily adapts to crowds of different sizes. The key is building the walls at an appropriate sitting height: 14 in. to 16 in. is ideal, although slightly shorter or taller walls will suffice.

Capping the walls off with a smooth layer of stone, brick, wood, or tile will make them more comfortable and prevent clothing from being snagged. Mixing materials—such as brick walls with a bluestone cap, stucco walls with a tile cap, or river-rock walls with a flagstone cap—can make a seating wall especially eye-catching. Building the walls 12 in. to 16 in. wide will give them appropriate visual weight in the landscape while ensuring a comfy seating surface.

▲ BECAUSE THE FLOORING is so visually dominant, seating was placed along the edges of this garden patio. While the red garden bench makes this space compelling for one or two people, the flagstone retaining walls embracing the patio can seat nearly a dozen partygoers.

Porches

THE PRIMARY DRAWING CARD OF PORCHES (often called porticos) is that they provide shelter from the weather—whether the blazing sun in summer, showers during the rainy season, or wind in exposed settings. Although they complement almost any architectural style, porches are most common in temperate regions. Some, such as those in the American Southwest, are built at ground level. Others, like those in the Deep South, may be raised several feet aboveground.

Because they offer shelter, porches can be treated much like indoor rooms and outfitted with furniture, lamps, carpets, and other accessories. Even media centers may be built into these outdoor structures. While outdoor-grade furnishings will weather best, especially in humid climates, indoor-grade furnishings can often be used successfully if located against interior walls. Lighting, ceiling fans, and an outdoor sound system will enhance any porch, making it the perfect place to entertain rain or shine.

◄ THIS BACK PORCH features cut-stone floors instead of traditional wood floors. It is also enclosed by a stone wall instead of wooden balustrades. The stone visually unifies the home with the walls and structures in the surrounding landscape.

▶ BRIGHT COLORS AND CREATIVE MILLWORK in the eaves, columns, balustrades, and newel posts give this Victorian-style porch character and create a welcoming spot for casual conversation. Paint, materials, and millwork can also be chosen to complement porches on contemporary, traditional, Craftsman, and other styles of homes.

▲ THIS PORCH IS BROAD ENOUGH to create a roomlike setting with seating arranged in a conversational grouping. Porches 8 ft. to 12 ft. wide are necessary for this type of seating arrangement; those 6 ft. wide are better suited for a row of rockers or chairs.

▶ WHEN SITTING ON THE FRONT PORCH, these homeowners can converse with neighbors out for an evening walk or watch children playing in adjacent yards. The porch also provides a nice setting for greeting guests and bidding them a friendly farewell.

▼ A COMBINATION OF AFFORDABLE indoor and outdoor furnishings creates a safari-like setting beneath the eave of this porch. A trunk doubles as an occasional table and storage unit, while a tall screen helps hide a grill tucked in the corner. Camouflage curtains soften the walls.

PORCH STYLES

House

GALLEY PORCH

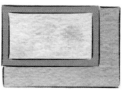

WRAPAROUND PORCH

EXTENDED PORCH

ALCOVE PORCH

CORNER PORCH

▲ PAINTING A PORCH CEILING A SOFT COLOR helps create a relaxed outdoor environment. The powdery blue-gray paint on this ceiling (which, according to legend, is said to keep evil spirits at bay) is echoed in the floor and seating to create a sense of unity.

▲ WRAPAROUND PORCHES, by their very design, create at least two outdoor areas—one on either side of the corner. The space on the side shown here can comfortably seat a small family, providing a spot for conversation, board games, or reading a good book.

Let the Music Play

ANY GATHERING BENEFITS from a background of music. Indoor sound systems can be wired with weatherproof outdoor speakers that sit on shelves, mount on walls, recess into ceilings, or are placed discreetly in the landscape.

Most sound systems will allow you to switch between A and B settings for indoor or outdoor music, while many newer systems let you create multiple sound zones with different music at different decibel levels playing at the same time.

Multiple small speakers located throughout the landscape will produce higher quality sound than two speakers covering a large area but may require the assistance of a sound professional for installation and compliance with building codes.

▲ BY CONTINUING THE DRY-LAID STONE SURFACE from the porch onto the adjacent patio without a change in grade, a continuous outdoor living area is formed in both sun and shade. The rusty red color of the furniture, pots, and stone helps visually connect the space.

◄ WITH PORCHES ON ALL FOUR CORNERS, this house is filled with light as the sun moves across the sky. Four porches also enable the homeowners to create individual outdoor spaces suited to different types of entertaining and activities.

Plantings with Purpose

PLANTS ARE A NATURAL PART OF ANY OUTDOOR LIVING SPACE—**whether** grown in beds, containers, or window boxes—but all too often, they are an impulse purchase or afterthought. With a bit of planning, however, plants can be used to create atmosphere, change the conditions of an outdoor setting, provide screening, or enhance specific views.

Culinary herbs and vegetables, for instance, can be conveniently grown close to the kitchen. Soothing foliage plants can enhance quiet areas designed for relaxing, while brightly colored flowers will energize spaces for entertaining, and fragrant plants will enhance any setting. Trees and vines can be used to create shade, evergreen shrubs can provide privacy, and ornamental grasses will shimmer in sunlight when placed to the southwest of a sitting area.

Plants with colorful fall foliage should be planted near the rooms enjoyed most in autumn, while plants with evergreen foliage or striking bark, berries, and branching patterns should be positioned near windows for winter enjoyment.

▲ THIS PORCH IS ORIENTED to provide shade on sunny days. Orientation can also determine how much sun and wind a porch receives, as well as whether it offers views of the sunrise or sunset—important considerations if the space will be used for entertaining.

▲ ADDING AN AWNING OVERHEAD and providing continuous paving underfoot extends this narrow porch into a larger area suitable for outdoor living. The bold foliage plants help bring life to the space and create a relaxed atmosphere.

▼ IN HOT CLIMATES, high ceilings allow the heat to rise, while ceiling fans generate a breeze even on still days. The light colors on these walls and in the seat cushions reflect rather than absorb heat, ensuring family and friends are always comfortable.

▲ PORCHES, BECAUSE OF THEIR PROXIMITY TO INDOOR ROOMS, often serve as overflow spaces when entertaining. Guests enjoy being able to step outside for fresh air or quiet conversation. This porch, outfitted with a comfortable sofa, is ideal for such an occasion.

▲ THIS HOME FEATURES A SERIES of outdoor patios, decks, and porches that serve as key transitional areas between indoors and out, that can be used in different seasons, and that are connected to improve circulation when entertaining.

▶ THE PALMS PLANTED AROUND THE BASE of this porch provide a see-through screen that forms a cozy, protected setting while still letting in lots of light, encouraging conversation with passersby, and offering views of the neighborhood.

◄ BY PLACING A FEW CHAIRS just beyond this door, guests are encouraged to linger a little longer before heading home after a visit. This strategy works equally well on front, back, and side porches, depending on which is most frequently used by close friends.

▲ TWIG FURNITURE, which would tend to rot quickly in the garden unless frequently sealed, will last much longer beneath a sheltered eave. Accompanied by an eclectic mix of rustic furnishings, this charming nook is an ideal spot for tea, lunch, or a short visit with friends.

◄ A FLAIR FOR CREATIVITY can do more than the most generous budgets. Colorful, billowing curtains and oversized throw pillows create a casual environment equally suited for adults or teens. The rod-mounted curtains can be easily adjusted to block the sun's glare.

Decks

WHETHER UP IN THE TREETOPS ON A HILLSIDE LOT or just a few feet above the ground on a flat site, decks can be adapted to nearly any property. They may be constructed in various configurations and can be easily added or expanded after a home has been built. On steep lots, a series of cascading decks make excellent use of otherwise unusable space and create multiple areas for congregating. On level lots, decks may be little more than low wooden platforms, but even this subtle change in grade adds dimension to an otherwise flat yard.

Decks can be enhanced with unique railings, creative flooring patterns, or an arbor for shade. They can also incorporate an existing landscape feature, such as a prized tree, by being built to surround or blend in with it. Accent lighting and decorative furnishings can easily transform a deck into the perfect outdoor-entertaining area.

▼ THIS SIMPLE, OPEN DECK DESIGN echoes the clean lines and low profile of the house, allowing it to sit discreetly in an environment that has been preserved for the most part, rather than cleared for lawns and landscaping. The steps down to the deck follow the natural terrain.

▲ LARGE DECKS ARE GREAT FOR ENTER-
TAINING, and this one can handle a
crowd. With its mix of chairs, chaises,
and table seating, the deck can support
the variety of activities likely to take
place when family and friends gather
for a weekend at the lake.

◄ THIS LOW DECK WRAPS AROUND THE
HOUSE, making a subtle transition between house and garden and improv-
ing circulation. Built-in lights placed
every few feet along the deck's edge
make it safe and easy to move about
when enjoying the outdoors at night.

▲ DECKS GET A LOT OF USE because they are accessible. The challenge is ensuring that seating areas don't impede traffic flow. The best solution is to create a cul-de-sac for the furniture off to one side of the door, which also helps to increase privacy.

► ALTHOUGH THIS DECK LACKS SHELTER, it is still decorated comfortably and practically. Blankets, rugs, and ornamental accents may need to be stashed in a nearby closet when rain threatens, but weather-resistant outdoor-wicker furniture can be left outside all season long.

Use Containers to Define Spaces

CONTAINER PLANTINGS CAN DO MORE THAN ADD A SPOT OF COLOR or soften hard land-scaping features. Two large pots placed 4 ft. apart can create a doorway. Several pots lined up in a row can define a wall. Clustered pots of varied sizes can mark a corner. By combining these placement strategies, pots can define an entire outdoor room, whether a patio, a small section of a deck, or a garden room in one area of the lawn.

For best results, use large pots and plants with bold foliage; the large pots will reduce watering requirements, and the bold foliage will provide long-season interest. Choose evergreen foliage for year-round staying power, and include flowering plants for a touch of color and fragrance.

▲ ALTHOUGH THE TEAK TABLE AND CHAIRS are located on a large deck, the dining area feels like a small room because it has been partially enclosed with container plantings. The plantings also dress up the space with texture and color.

▲ PLANTINGS WERE BROUGHT ALL THE WAY UP to the edge of this low deck, emphasizing the garden atmosphere. Building codes often allow low decks to be built without railings as long as the deck height doesn't exceed local standards.

◄ LARGE SHEETS OF CLEAR PLEXIGLAS® have been mounted between posts at the corner of this deck to provide a windscreen for the dining table without hampering views. Where privacy outranks views, windscreens can be created with trees, hedges, fences, and walls.

▼ THIS OUTDOOR AREA IS PART PORCH and part deck, as defined by the striking roof beams, which are only partially covered by a roof. By creating areas in both sun and shade, this deck is made more versatile and appealing throughout the day and seasons.

▲ THE SOLID RAILING ON THIS DECK increases privacy in an urban setting without making the space feel closed in. The clean lines and materials of the railing complement the contemporary architecture of the house, creating a chic space for a nightcap with friends.

Relating Indoors and Out

WHEN DESIGNING OUTDOOR SPACES, start indoors. Determine the kinds of gathering spots most suitably connected to interior rooms: a dining area just outside the kitchen, an area for entertaining beyond the living room, or a space to linger with guests near the front door.

Look out the windows and doors: Identify views to preserve and screen; determine where focal points would make the strongest statement; and make note of sun and shade patterns that should be capitalized on or altered.

Finally, identify visual design elements used indoors—colors, textures, decorative elements, or flooring materials—that might be repeated outdoors to create a sense of unity.

▲ THE STURDY, WROUGHT-IRON ARBOR over this deck is covered with wisteria— a fragrant, deciduous vine that provides light shade in warm weather but allows sunlight to shine through In cooler seasons when it loses its leaves.

▲ SECTIONS OF SAILCLOTH HAVE BEEN STRUNG between this house and posts to create an overhead canopy that cuts the sun's harshest rays while still allowing ample light on this deck and terrace. Sailcloth is a sturdy material that holds up well to wind and rain.

Low-Care, Long-Wear Decking

EXPOSED WOOD FLOORS TAKE A BEATING from sun, rain, and wind, so durable decking materials are essential. Pressure-treated lumber (choose an arsenic-free product) is the most affordable option, but it must be sealed every other year and has a limited life expectancy.

Naturally rot-resistant woods, such as cedar, redwood, and sustainably harvested tropical hardwoods, are more expensive but last longer and weather beautifully without sealants.

Composite decking materials, as well as metal and vinyl decking systems, are long lasting, rot- and insect-resistant, free of splinters, and easier to maintain than wood. But choose carefully among these new materials; a few may look artificial or may not be approved by local building codes.

BENCH WITH A BACKREST

A built-in bench with a backrest can double as a deck railing.

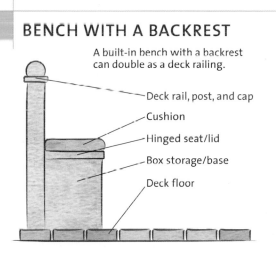

Deck rail, post, and cap

Cushion

Hinged seat/lid

Box storage/base

Deck floor

▲ ALLOW FOR AN ASSORTMENT OF PLACES for snacks during a party so that guests can mingle through the whole entertaining space. Here, a variety of occasional and dining tables provide plenty of places to nibble and chat.

◀ WITH ENOUGH ATTENTION TO DETAIL, decks can be designed as significant architectural features of a house. This one has an elegant curved shape and a unique railing that makes it as beautiful to look at as it is to look out from.

Relaxing and Escaping

With today's fast pace of living, everyone needs a place to relax—somewhere to simply be and not do. No place is better suited for unwinding than home, but it helps to designate a space away from the telephone, television, home office, laundry room, and other activity areas.

Whether it's a screened porch, rooftop oasis, garden getaway, or backyard spa, a well-designed retreat incorporates the elements that its users find most relaxing. For some, that means a comfortable chair surrounded by lush foliage and soft music. Others may prefer a rocking chair on a balcony or a float drifting in the pool. Regardless, soothing colors, natural textures, soft light, and the sounds of chirping birds, trickling fountains, or whirring ceiling fans are all good bets for lowering your blood pressure.

Spaces in which to stretch out and nap—a sleeping porch, hammock, or sofa with a light throw—are especially appealing. However, some people find that escaping the stresses of daily life is best achieved by being active in a relaxing way. Backyard workshops, studios, and greenhouses are ideal for such pursuits. Lounging around an outdoor hearth, soaking in a therapeutic spa, or showering au natural can also do the trick.

◄ THIS PORCH STRIKES A BALANCE between the architectural formality of the house and a comfortable outdoor setting. Architectural elements with exterior exposures are stained white to match the house trim. The rafter ceiling, timber mantel, and stone-veneered fireplace introduce natural materials.

Screened Porches and Sunrooms

SCREENED PORCHES ALLOW YOU TO EXPERIENCE the fresh air, cool breezes, and soothing sounds of nature while offering protection from the summer sun, seasonal rains, and pesky insects. A 300-sq.-ft. to 400-sq.-ft. porch offers ample space for relaxing and dining, and a rectangular floor plan offers greater design flexibility than a square one. When a porch is added to an existing house, it's important for it to blend in with the architecture. Painting or staining the wood to match the house or trim color, as well as adding architectural details used in the house, will create a sense of unity.

Similar in size and location to screened porches, sunrooms are light-filled spaces that can be enjoyed year-round. Surrounded by glass, they extend visually into the landscape yet may be heated or cooled for comfort. They are excellent places to grow houseplants, host a small luncheon, or curl up with a good book.

◄ LOCATED WELL ABOVE THE TREETOPS, this upper-level porch offers excellent views of the coast. High ceilings add to the spacious atmosphere but still offer shelter from the rain and sun. Screened walls allow gentle breezes to pass through, while helping to moderate wind gusts.

► THIS VACATION HOME IN THE BLUE RIDGE MOUNTAINS is half porch, half deck, providing the owners with multiple spaces for outdoor living. A broad front porch and rear deck flank a generous screened porch with a stacked-stone fireplace for relaxing outdoors even on chilly days.

◄ THE DOOR LEADING FROM THIS
PORCH to the outside stoop is cleverly
designed to match the broad, screened
wall panels; only the door handle and
automatic-closing device give it away.
The porch trim is painted forest green
to match the house and deck trim.

Designing Porch Walls

To MAXIMIZE THE OUTDOOR
ATMOSPHERE, **screen**
porch walls from floor to
ceiling. For a roomlike setting, enclose the lower
section with bead board
or other siding. As an
alternative, sandwich the
screen between decorative
trim to create a semi-
enclosed lower wall with
architectural character.

▲ NOT ALL PORCHES HAVE WOOD FLOORS, although additional structural support may be required for stone, brick, or tile floors. The mortared flagstone on this porch adds visual warmth and character, and it also ties the room to the surrounding landscape.

◀ SINCE ALL OF THE JOINTS in a porch are exposed rather than hidden behind walls, precision construction is important. This porch features many finely executed curved details—rounded corner brackets, rafter tips, and cap rails atop the solid wall.

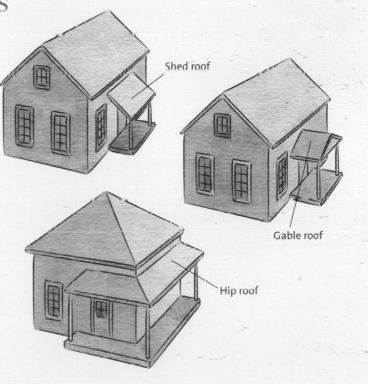

◀ THIS DECK WAS DESIGNED as a quiet retreat in the treetops. The simplicity of furnishings helps create a contemplative environment for reading or a nap, and the clean lines of the building materials visually connect this space to the house.

Protective Porch Roofs

PORCH ROOFS HAVE TWO ROLES: They should visually unite a porch with the architecture of the home and protect the porch from the elements. Although shed roofs are common, easy to build, and complement farmhouse architecture, hip and gable roofs offer greater protection from the weather and complement a wider range of architectural styles.

Hip roofs overhang on all sides, screening the sun in hot climates and providing the greatest protection from rain. Gable roofs allow more natural light onto porches and feature an attractive triangular roofline, but they provide slightly less protection from sun and rain than hip roofs. For this reason, gable-roofed porches should not face west—the direction from which hard, blowing rains typically prevail.

Shed roof

Gable roof

Hip roof

◄ CAREFUL ATTENTION TO DETAILING results in an outdoor room as attractive as any indoor room. Sealed hardwood floors—rather than the usual painted, stained, or natural flooring planks—enhance this porch, which gives it the polished look of an interior space.

▼ THE 12-IN. BOXED COLUMNS on this porch feature white-stained crown molding, base molding, and decorative railing. The columns not only look great, but also carefully conceal wiring and support electrical outlets that are used for floor lamps.

Lighting a Porch

WHILE CEILING FIXTURES ARE THE MOST COMMON LIGHTING used on a porch, they aren't always the most practical. Because there are no roof cavities in which to hide can-light fixtures, choices are limited to exterior mount and hanging fixtures. Also, overhead lights rarely create the soft ambient light that is so appealing on a porch.

Floor lamps, table lamps, and wall sconces create much softer lighting, but some advanced planning is required for their installation. Prerouting porch posts before construction will allow wiring for light fixtures and electrical outlets to be concealed from view. Header beams can also be prerouted and wired to an electrical switch so that festive string lights can be mounted overhead.

▼ PORCH ADDITIONS LOOK BEST if they are designed to look like part of the home's original architecture rather than as an "enclosed deck." The Prairie-style windows help accomplish that here, as do the boards that enclose the open space beneath the deck.

◀ THIS TRADITIONAL, WOOD-FRAMED CONSERVATORY with glass windows was added to the house to create an elegant sunroom. This sunroom has a glass ceiling, making it an especially bright room for dining, reading, or tending houseplants. Swinging windows allow fresh air inside.

▼ WHEN THESE HOMEOWNERS REALIZED THAT ADDING a screened porch to their house would block light in the living room, they opted for a freestanding porch that includes an upstairs studio. It flows out onto a dry-laid stone patio that connects the house and porch.

▲ THE COMBINATION OF THE BARREL-VAULTED CEILING and flat, dropped ceilings break up this large space, creating sheltered areas for dining and sitting while drawing attention to the mountain view beyond. Broad eaves provide shelter from rainstorms.

◄ TRANSOM WINDOWS, exposed timber rafters, and a vaulted ceiling give this sunroom a sense of height and help form a bright, airy space. The wainscot and uplights draw the eye upward, while the dark tile floors ground the room and give it a sense of warmth.

Balconies and Rooftops

BALCONIES AND ROOFTOPS ARE RARELY SHELTERED, **but** like porches and sunrooms, they offer quiet refuges just steps away from a home's interior living spaces. Balconies are frequently located near bedrooms, so an east or west orientation appropriately affords a view of the sunrise or sunset. They may either extend from the house or be recessed into a nook.

Rooftop patios, while most common above in-town lofts, row houses, or other flat-roofed city buildings, are welcome in any environment where interesting views abound. Although creating a garden on a rooftop usually requires hauling lots of pots, plants, bags of soil, and furnishings up staircases, the results can be well worth the effort—a lush urban oasis from which to enjoy a romantic dinner beneath the stars. Arbors and other garden structures can even be built to create a shady rooftop retreat if desired. Just use sturdy materials and anchor them securely to the roof because they will occasionally be exposed to fierce winds.

▲ BALCONIES ARE USUALLY SMALLER than decks and located off private upstairs quarters, making them excellent places to begin and end the day. The railing on this balcony is just high enough to create a safe environment while permitting views to the bay beyond.

◄ EVEN CITY DWELLERS CAN ENJOY their own outdoor "private" space. The surrounding building walls cast shade and buffer the wind on this rooftop, creating a variable, changing environment, while container plants help green up the space.

▲ SIMPLE, COZY BALCONIES can be added to many rooms without breaking the budget. This one, built just off a master bedroom, is perfect for a couple to unwind before turning in for the night.

Backyard Retreats

EVERYONE NEEDS SPACE IN WHICH TO ESCAPE, if ever so briefly, from the hustle and bustle of daily activities. Depending on your idea of "getting away," a backyard retreat could take the form of a simple garden bench, a Japanese-style teahouse, or an artist's studio. And every landscape, regardless of size, can benefit from a quiet seating area. Whether a teak bench overlooking a pond or a conversation nook in a garden, designating a special spot to unwind will enhance your outdoor experience.

Gazebos and pergolas provide sheltered areas that offer a peaceful sense of enclosure and sanctuary from the outside world. As large structures, they often double as focal points in the landscape. Garages, playhouses, sheds, and custom-built structures can be transformed into studios or workshops and can afford the mental and physical space to really relax. Regardless of what form your ideal retreat takes, comfortable furnishings will ensure that the space is as rejuvenating and versatile as you wish it to be.

▲ RATHER THAN PLACE THIS BENCH randomly along a garden path, it was neatly tucked in among the foliage—making it every bit as important to the garden composition as any of the plants. It provides a quiet place to pause while wandering through the garden.

◄ DUBBED THE "HOLLY HOUSE" by its owners because architectural features and paint colors mimic the leaves and berries of nearby holly bushes, this freestanding structure is a screened porch in the woods where the family can get out of the house without going too far.

▲ LANDSCAPING SLOPED SITES can be challenging, as structures require solid foundations, and access trails call for carefully placed steps. Here, a large pavilion was built on a steep hillside overlooking a waterfall. It was carefully tucked into the woods to avoid disturbing too many trees.

GAZEBOS AND PERGOLAS

▲ THE OCTAGONAL FAÇADE,
turreted roof, and arched openings
make this screened gazebo a focal
point in the backyard. The siding,
trim, and roofing materials match
those of the house, lending a
sense of unity to the landscape.

◀ PERGOLAS WERE ORIGINALLY
DESIGNED as covered passageways but
quickly evolved into destinations of
their own. This pergola spans a raised
walkway, yet it is wide enough for a
couple of wicker rockers, which offer an
excellent viewing point in the garden.

▲ WINDOWPANES ADD TO THE ROOMLIKE ATMOSPHERE
of this pergola. The entire structure is tucked neatly into a
mixed shrub and perennial border, making it a favorite garden
getaway, as well as a place for the gardener to take a short break.

▲ NESTLED IN A WOODLAND GARDEN, the temperature in this gazebo is considerably cooler than in the sun on a hot summer day. The roof provides shelter from sun and rain, while a latticed section helps keep shrubs from reaching into the sitting area.

▶ ALTHOUGH NOT VERY COMMON TODAY, gazebos—structures originally designed for gazing—are often built in the form of turrets, echoing architectural elements of an accompanying home. The sides of this gazebo are designed to look like large windows for gazing.

▶ THIS ASIAN-STYLE PAVILION is not overly large, yet it easily accommodates six chairs around a central table. Side-panel drapes can be closed for added privacy or to provide screening from light breezes or unexpected rain showers.

▼ THIS WELL-PROPORTIONED and thoughtfully detailed gazebo is small enough to tuck into an urban backyard but large enough to seat four for dinner or a game of cards. The decorative railing, corner brackets, shingled roof, and cupola make it an eye-catching addition to the landscape.

Upgrading Gazebo Floors

GAZEBO FLOORS ARE MOST COMMONLY constructed from decking wood, but flagstone, tile, brick, or concrete pavers laid on a slab can also be used. They require minimal maintenance and will remain beautiful for years. Decorative concrete that has been stained or textured can provide character.

▶ STRIKING REFLECTIONS CAN BE CREATED by placing architectural structures near water features with dark interiors. The combo here works in concert to provide stunning views and a soothing setting that is conducive to quiet activities. The old tree contributes to this scene.

▼ TODAY'S GARDEN STRUCTURES are often hybrids of pergolas, arbors, pavilions, and gazebos—incorporating the best elements of each. This open-roofed structure, which spans a deck, clearly defines a casual area for dining and enjoying the views, while providing support for flowering vines.

▲ ANYTHING WHITE IN THE LANDSCAPE is the first thing to catch the eye—so this gazebo is, appropriately, the focal point of the backyard garden. Two intricately pruned topiaries mark the entrance to the gazebo, keeping with the formal design of the structure.

Keeping Cool

ALTHOUGH PERGOLAS, GAZEBOS, AND PAVILIONS ARE OFTEN ADDED for their structural and aesthetic contributions to a landscape, their original purpose, dating back to Roman times, was to provide a cool place to relax on a hot day. While the structures themselves offer some shade, their cooling abilities can be enhanced by adding a solid roof (which also sheds rain), creating a leafy canopy overhead with dense vines, or adding ceiling fans.

Shading south- and west-facing walls with lattice or dense plantings can also help lower temperatures by as much as 10°F on a hot summer day. By building pergolas adjacent to a house, indoor temperatures can be lowered, too.

GARDEN SEATING

▲ BENCHES MADE OF NATURAL MATERIALS blend almost seamlessly into the landscape. This one was made from large stone slabs, but a single large boulder or even a tree stump would provide an equally enchanting place to pause while exploring the garden.

▲ BENCHES CAN BE PLACED along the edge of a lawn like this one, along a path, or overlooking a special view. Because this bench accommodates a basket of flowers, it encourages sitting alone rather than with family or friends.

▶ A SITTING AREA WAS CREATED in this garden by simply widening the path by a few feet. The rustic twig furniture maintains the naturalistic feel, but it can be uncomfortable; weatherproof fabric cushions solve this problem, while adding pattern and color that complement the plantings.

▲ A CONVERSATION NOOK with garden benches and chairs was created in this small boxwood parterre, or patterned garden. Although it is located adjacent to the house, it is out of the main flow of traffic, ensuring a quiet place to relax.

Creating the Perfect Sitting Area

DIFFERENT PEOPLE LIKE SITTING IN DIFFERENT ENVIRONMENTS. Some enjoy the warmth of the sun; others prefer a shady canopy. Some embrace open spaces with expansive views; others settle more comfortably into cozy nooks. Some like feeling as if they are sitting on top of the world; others seek the security of a sunken garden.

Before settling on the location for a seating area, try this trick: Each day, place a folding chair in a different location, sit there awhile, and take note of how it feels. Keep moving the chair around until you find just the right spot for a more permanent bench or cluster of chairs.

► LIKE MOST COZY SEATING AREAS, this one has a backdrop and sense of enclosure. The rough stone retaining wall also provides a striking counterpoint to the smooth surface of the teak benches. As the Latin inscription on the chairs proclaims: "Behold how good." Indeed!

▼ NATURALLY ROT-RESISTANT WOODS such as teak, cedar, and redwood are good choices for benches that will remain outside year round. The design of this teak bench is particularly suitable for the contemporary house style and casual landscape.

STUDIOS, WORKSHOPS & TEAHOUSES

◀ THIS OPEN-AIR BEDROOM was built at the end of a deck, beneath—and around—towering cedars and hemlocks, and enclosed by lush evergreen shrubs. The sleeping shelter was wired for lighting, making it usable in the nighttime as well as during the day.

▶ THIS JAPANESE-STYLE PAVILION overlooks a small koi pond, creating a serene destination and making the most of a compact, fenced backyard. The unusual roof design allows light to shine through the windows at either end of the roof peak, while easily shedding rain.

▶ THIS BACKYARD RETREAT features a carved wooden door rescued from a salvage yard and wooden posts made from the only two trees removed during the building's construction. It serves as a center for gardening activities and provides a convenient place to store garden tools.

▲ TREE HOUSES ARE EXPERIENCING a resurgence of interest among both adults and children. This sturdily crafted structure is built around multiple tree trunks and features a gathering room with a wood-burning fireplace and a loft accessed by a ladder. It is wired for electricity.

▶ THIS GREENHOUSE is both elegant and functional. Contrasting with the formal design and dressy chandelier are an informal, dry-laid brick floor that allows water to seep through and a functional potting bench with under-counter storage for pots, potting soil, and amendments.

A Gardener's Refuge

Gardeners have different ways of going about their activities, but all tend to establish a home base around which all activities revolve. It may take the form of a potting shed or greenhouse, a mudroom just inside the back door, a freestanding storage shed, a corner of the garage, or a potting bench tucked beneath an eave.

Regardless of its form or location, a gardener's work space will benefit from shelter overhead, a work counter built at standing height, storage shelves and hooks, access to running water, and a shady spot for holding plants. It helps to keep wheelbarrows, buckets, shovels, and other gardening tools near at hand.

▼ THIS GARDEN HOUSE was built on a raised platform that creates a deck around the small outbuilding, making the space multifunctional. More than a half dozen container plantings were clustered at the corner to visually connect the building to its natural surroundings.

◄ ALTHOUGH THIS GREENHOUSE RE-CEIVES FULL SUN in winter, it is shaded by a mass of morning glories in summer that helps it to blend seamlessly into the surrounding garden. It serves as a center for year-round gardening activities.

◀ GARDEN PATHS ARE MUCH MORE COMPELLING when they lead somewhere that can only be glimpsed in the distance. This woodland path leads to a sheltered seating area made of redwood and stone. The trickling stream nearby contributes to the soothing setting.

▼ THIS JAPANESE-STYLE TEAHOUSE features stucco walls and a shake roof that echo the design of the surrounding garden walls. Built-in benches offer a sheltered place to sit and enjoy the koi pond even in inclement weather.

A Rainy Day Escape

AN OUTDOOR STRUCTURE can be an enchanting place to spend a warm, rainy afternoon. Larger spaces or those with broad roof eaves will stay drier than small spaces, as will those with partial enclosures, wind breaks, or curtains that can be drawn when there's a slight breeze.

Making the Most of Natural Light

MANY BACKYARD BUILDINGS rely solely on natural light. But even when wired for electricity, ample natural light will make a studio, cottage, workshop, or shed more inviting. When designing an outdoor building, start by positioning the windows to capture the most desirable light, which will be dictated by when the space is most likely to be used.

Include oversized windows and windowed doors, adding shades or sheers, if necessary, to filter the light during the brightest times of day. Add skylights to flood the interior with overhead light. And finally, paint the walls a light color to help bounce light around the room; a light-colored ceiling also brightens the atmosphere.

▲ SITUATED JUST BEYOND THE BACK DOOR, this working greenhouse offers the ultimate in convenience to home and garden. It was carefully designed to complement the house—down to the double-hung windows and stained, shingle siding.

► SOMETIMES BACKYARD RETREATS ARE TEMPORARY—designed for certain seasons or special occasions. An outdoor bed might not be practical in the rainy season, but it is a novel place to lounge in fair weather. Colorful rugs, throws, and pillows help create an exotic setting.

▲ THIS RAISED RETREAT offers aerial views of the expansive surrounding gardens. The tropical plantings, as well as the exotic architecture and decorative accents, transport the homeowners from their Pacific Northwest backyard to places they visited a half a world away.

Warm Hearths

NOTHING KNOCKS THE CHILL OFF A COOL EVENING faster than a blazing fire. In fact, outdoor hearths can be even more inviting than indoor hearths because temperature swings are greater outdoors. Outdoor hearths create the kind of ambience that transforms a typical evening into a memorable one, and they can extend the season for outdoor living.

Outdoor hearths come in all shapes and sizes—from fire pits, fire dishes, chimineas, and luminaries to full-sized and oversized fireplaces with mantels, raised hearths, and chimneys. They may be custom built on site, installed as modular prefabricated components, or delivered as ready-to-light units. For porches and sunrooms with interior walls, vent-free fireplaces are an appealing option. Finishing materials run the gamut from stone, brick, and stucco to colorful, decorative tile. Fuel sources include wood and gas, as well as alternative fuels such as wax-based logs, pellets, and gels.

▶ THIS RUSTIC STONE FIREPLACE shares a chimney with an indoor fireplace—a smart money-saving strategy. A ledge was built into the brick firebox, allowing a grilling rack to be placed over the fire for cooking.

▼ IN WARM CLIMATES, a fireplace is more for ambience than warmth, but it can knock off the chill on a damp day. These vented gas logs are a good choice, as they look like burning logs but put out less heat than ventless logs or firewood.

◀ THIS CUSTOM-BUILT STUCCO FIREPLACE doubles as a patio wall, defining one boundary of an outdoor room. Built-in storage bins keep firewood dry and convenient. This area, with the formal fireplace, traditional seating arrangement, and patterned floor, demonstrates how you can capture an indoor feeling outdoors.

▲ FIREWOOD IS CONVENIENTLY STACKED to the right of this fireplace. Allowed to dry for six months, the wood will light easily and burn hot. If well-seasoned wood isn't available, wax-based fire logs, which reduce emissions by up to two-thirds, are a smart environmental alternative.

◄ RECTANGULAR SPACES OFFER GREATER FLEXIBILITY for arranging furniture. The size and shape of this space allows for two seating areas—a warm conversation area near the fireplace, plus a nearby dining area that still benefits from the ambience created by the fireplace.

▼ A GAS-FUELED FIRE PIT warms this patio seating area, which offers all the comforts of informality while still being chic. A wooden bench and Adirondack chairs have been pulled up around the fire pit as if it were a campfire, forming a casual conversation area.

Evolution of the Modern Fireplace

TRADITIONAL MASONRY FIREPLACES are going the way of the dinosaur as more affordable, energy-efficient models made from premanufactured modular masonry sections take their place. Another new option, a wood-framed fireplace with metal firebox and chimney, is even more affordable but less energy efficient than a modular masonry fireplace.

Both styles are widely available, easily installed, and offer a choice of wood-burning, direct-vent gas, and vent-free gas units. Vent-free models, built with technology similar to that of gas stoves, are good choices where it would be difficult to build a chimney. The fireplace surrounds on all models may be dressed up with brick, stone, tile, or stucco.

◄ THIS OUTDOOR ROOM is located in a courtyard pavilion that has solid walls along two sides. This wall features a fireplace with a stone façade and hearth that imitate the look of an indoor room. An outdoor kitchen is built into the adjoining wall.

▲ THIS PORTABLE FIRE PIT burns either charcoal or small logs. It is ideal for tight spaces and can be easily moved to a new location. The rounded cover acts as a fire screen, and a grill rack can be laid on top for cooking.

► A FREESTANDING STUCCO FIREPLACE is built into a curved seating wall, making it the focal point of the backyard patio and an inviting place to gather around. Candles can be placed on the recessed and stone-ledge shelves for added ambience and soft lighting.

▲ IN-GROUND AND CONTAINER GARDENS with roses, herbs, and citrus trees partially enclose this generous brick patio to create a relaxed atmosphere around the fireplace. A separate area for dining is located nearby, adjacent to both indoor and outdoor kitchens.

▲ THE STURDY, WISTERIA-DRAPED ARBOR helps identify the upper and outer boundaries of this outdoor room, which is anchored by a large, traditional masonry fireplace. The brick chimney extends slightly above the arbor, venting smoke away and preventing any harm to the vine.

▶ THE STONE USED IN THE FLOOR, walls, fireplace, and pool are the unifying element in this patio. The walls and fireplace, along with the painted arbor, define the seating area, while the pool contributes to a relaxing atmosphere. The walls provide ample seating when entertaining.

Heat Where You Need It

A PRACTICAL AND AFFORDABLE ALTERNATIVE to fireplaces and fire pits is the patio heater. Fueled by either natural gas or propane, patio heaters come in tabletop and floor models and with stainless steel or painted finishes. Most have adjustable heat output and easy-to-use ignition starters. Look for a sturdy model with safety valves that shut off the unit automatically if it is tilted.

Patio heaters are designed primarily for use in open spaces. If used beneath a structure, be sure there is a high, flame-retardant roof overhead and excellent ventilation. Patio heaters may be connected to natural gas lines or fueled with propane tanks for greater portability.

▶ IF YOU DON'T HAVE THE SPACE, budget, or inclination for an outdoor hearth but want the heating benefits, consider a portable heater. This one burns natural gas. It has a heavy base to prevent it from tipping over and a flared cap that radiates heat in a 20-ft. radius. Smaller tabletop models, as well as propane models, are also available.

▲ A BROAD BRICK FIREPLACE doubles as a retaining wall along the hillside. The wall also offers built-in cabinets and bluestone counters that can be used for gardening or entertaining needs. The brick chimney is just high enough to direct smoke away from the patio.

▶ THIS GROUND-LEVEL FIRE PIT features two ring burners—round, steel pipes that can be connected to natural gas or propane and that are slightly buried beneath a nonflammable surface, such as gravel or lava rocks—to create a unique, multiflame effect.

▲ THE PAINTED WALLS, hardwood floors, and gas fireplace form a warm, comfortable setting on this porch that makes it feel like a family room. The wooden mantel and tile surround on the hearth add to the roomlike atmosphere, while ceiling fans keep warm air circulating.

◄ MODERN FIRE PITS, while diverse in style and character, are inspired by rustic council rings or campfire circles that were popular in the early 1900s as gathering places for song, dance, and storytelling. This one overlooks the surrounding countryside and features built-in seating.

▲ THE STACKED-STONE FIRE PIT matches the surrounding stone patio. Its circular shape is emphasized by the elegant, curved bench. The simple design and materials, as well as the mostly green, massed plantings, create a soothing atmosphere for relaxing around the fire.

◄ A SIMPLY CON-
STRUCTED FIRE PIT is
surrounded by a
round patio and a
rhododendron- and
azalea-filled garden.
It was constructed by
leaving a graveled
clearing in the center
of the patio, which is
encircled by rocks to
contain a small,
wood-burning fire.

▲ THIS BROAD STONE HEARTH offers casual seating
beneath a large pavilion, which is well suited for relaxed
gatherings with friends or family. The chimney for the
wood-burning fireplace extends outside and above the
pavilion to keep the space from filling with smoke.

◄ THE DECK FLOOR DOUBLES AS SEATING for this sunken
campfire area, located just a few feet from the outdoor
bedroom (the structure in the background). Wood-
burning fire pits are a good do-it-yourself weekend pro
ject for homeowners with basic masonry skills.

► THIS GAS-BURNING FIRE PIT anchors one corner of a small backyard patio. The stone in the raised fire pit matches that of the surrounding seat wall, as well as the stepping stones through the lawn. A high wall offers privacy in a neighborhood setting.

▼ KILN-FIRED, WOOD-BURNING CLAY CHIMINEAS are both affordable and ideal for small spaces. Because chimineas are portable, homeowners can take them along if they move, or they can be repositioned on decks, patios, or other open-air spaces for different occasions.

A Clean Burn

TRADITIONAL OPEN-COMBUSTION WOOD-BURNING FIREPLACES with their flickering flames and crackling sounds certainly offer the greatest ambience, but they aren't very energy efficient. Clean-burning and Environmental Protection Agency certified (FPA) wood-burning fireplaces—insulated, closed-combustion units with glass doors—put out more heat and generate less air pollution.

If watching flames through glass isn't your idea of ambience, burning well-seasoned firewood (dried for at least six months) or manufactured logs will help reduce wood smoke emissions. Traditional open-combustion fireplaces can be made more efficient by adding cast-iron or steel inserts that burn wood, natural gas, propane, pellets, or coal. Be sure to comply with any local regulations regarding fireplaces and fuels.

▼ SHARING A CHIMNEY with an indoor one, this fireplace features a uniquely shaped firebox opening. The surrounding white walls and dramatic arched entry form a bright and inviting courtyard setting that has been transformed into a striking outdoor room.

Soothing Spas

FEW OUTDOOR AMENITIES ARE AS RELAXING AS A SPA or hot tub. The warm water and pulsating jets soothe tired muscles and stimulate circulation—not to mention that they just feel good. Settling into a hot spa is a great way to warm up in cold weather, slow down before bedtime, or unwind with close friends after a long work week.

Spas come in a variety of models, from the traditional 1960s-style wooden hot tub and self-contained portable spas to custom in-ground, in-pool, and in-deck models. They feature a variety of seating arrangements, jet types and placement, and many extras such as built-in stereos, digital control panels, multicolored fiber-optic lighting, waterfall cascades, and built-in towel warmers. For greatest convenience, they should be placed either close to the house—perhaps just beyond the master bedroom or family room—or adjacent to a swimming pool.

▼ A SELF-CONTAINED PORTABLE SPA has been built into an attractive, reinforced deck with curving rails that overlooks the countryside. Deck spas can be positioned on the ground and surrounded by the decking. Otherwise, decks must be reinforced for the increased load.

◀ POURED-CONCRETE SPAS can be built in just about any shape. This spa's freeform shape, along with the surrounding rocks and lush plantings, helps it settle in visually with the neighboring fish pond, dry-laid stone patio, and tropical, hillside garden.

▲ SPAS CAN BE DESIGNED as part of a pool to save on construction and filtration costs, as well as to add an enhanced visual element to the pool. This raised spa features a cascade waterfall that flows into the swimming pool below.

▲ THIS SPA HAS BUILT-IN BENCH SEATING that can easily accommodate eight people. Bench seats are the standard for custom concrete spas. However, they are not as comfortable as the contoured seats in pre-fabricated spas, and they offer fewer options for jet placement.

▲ ACRYLIC SPAS, WHICH ARE WIDELY AVAILABLE and more economical than concrete spas, offer the greatest variety in seating, jet types, and jet placement. They also offer optional features—from cup holders, aromatherapy filters, and massaging foot rests to exercise gear and stereo systems.

▲ WHAT BETTER WAY TO RELAX than by settling into a soothing spa beneath the broad sky? This open setting permits cloud-watching by day and star-gazing by night, while nearby borders, which are anchored by evergreens, maintain a sense of privacy.

◄ WITH ITS TRIPLE CASCADE, this spa doubles as a recirculating water feature. It has been prominently positioned along a freestanding wall to serve as a focal point in the landscape. After relaxing in the water, spa-goers can dry off by the adjacent fire pit.

Creating Privacy

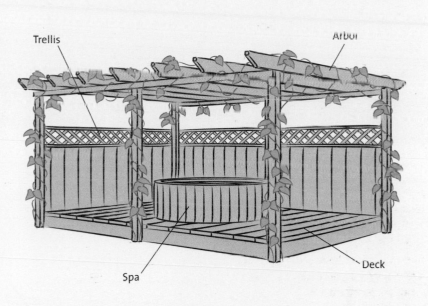

Trellis

Arbor

Spa

Deck

WHEN IT COMES TO SOAKING IN A SPA, most homeowners prefer a little privacy. Spas placed on a deck often end up in direct view of a neighboring house. If existing trees, shrubs, and fences don't provide enough privacy, consider building a trellis around the spa or deck. Planting it with evergreen vines will create a dense, year-round screen.

If the challenge is privacy from a two-story house towering nearby, an elegant and effective alternative is to build an arbor over the spa. Lattice can be added to one or more sides if needed for additional privacy, and large vines can be encouraged to scramble overhead.

▲ SPAS ARE MORE ENJOYABLE, and thus more frequently used, when a sense of privacy is ensured. This house and spa are set high on a hillside, so privacy is inherently provided. The prefabricated in-ground spa was situated to capture stunning sunrise views.

Open-Air Showers

OR MANY, AN OUTDOOR SHOWER CONJURES UP MEMORIES of the beach and rinsing the sand from feet and swimsuits before heading back into the house. But outdoor showers can also be part of an urban setting, providing a place to hose off your gardening clogs or even the dog.

Outdoor showers are a practical addition near a swimming pool, outside the back door, or just beyond the master bathroom. They can be built into a house wall or as separate units in the landscape, or they may be portable units hooked up to a garden hose. Unless they are used just for rinsing off or are built in a secluded location, outdoor showers need partial screening. (Total enclosure spoils the experience!) During the design process, provisions should be made for water access and adequate drainage. Towel bars, bath mats, and benches for clothing are much-appreciated amenities.

▶ INSTALLING A SHOWER against an exterior house wall offers an easy and affordable way to tap into water lines. This one is located just beyond the master bathroom and is used for washing off after a swim in the nearby lake or a soak in the spa.

▲ WHEN OUTDOOR SHOWERS ARE USED FOR BATHING, an enclosure built with rot-resistant, exterior-grade wood offers privacy. Benches, ledges, and hooks offer convenient spots to set down towels, hang swimsuits and clothing, or stash bathing necessities. Bath mats located just beyond the shower are also appreciated.

◄ SINCE THIS SHOWER IS USED FOR RINSING OFF before and after soaking in an in-ground spa, rather than for bathing outdoors, an enclosure was not necessary. The shower is tucked into a hedge to screen the wooden structure from view.

Portable Showers

AN OUTDOOR SHOWER DOESN'T HAVE TO BE FANCY OR EXPENSIVE—particularly if your goal is simply to rinse off after a swim in the pool or soak in the spa. Several inexpensive portable models that hook up to garden hoses are now commercially available. And with a little ingenuity, a homemade model can be constructed in an afternoon by using a showerhead, a faucet, a few pipes and connectors, and some kind of a stand.

▲ SINCE OUTDOOR SHOWERING is a warm-weather activity, the plumbing for this shower is kept simple. It consists of exposed pipes and hoses connected to an outdoor spigot that can be easily disconnected and drained before cold weather sets in.

▲ A PORTABLE SHOWER IS SITUATED at the corner of a deck next to a movable spa. It connects easily to a garden hose, but a faucet knob is provided on the shower post for convenience. A shower curtain can be pulled for privacy.

▲ FOR THOSE WHO PREFER hot baths to showers, an outdoor tub is the ultimate luxury in relaxation. In this novel setup, dense landscaping provides screening from neighboring properties, and the stone wall offers a place to set soap, towels, and a change of clothes.

▲ THIS PORCH SHOWER features copper wall panels, naturally rot-resistant cedar posts, and ipé (tropical hardwood) caps and decking. Decking is spaced to allow water to fall into a galvanized drain pan, where it is carried off to a dry well in the woods.

Outdoor Décor

A S THE CONCEPT OF OUTDOOR LIVING SPACES HAS EVOLVED over the past decade, exterior décor has followed suit. Outdoor rooms are being given the same design considerations as interior spaces, and the structural and decorative elements available to outfit them offer the same level of style and comfort that indoor rooms boast.

While garden structures are generally considered to be strictly utilitarian, they can also set the overall tone of an outdoor room by creating privacy, adding swaths of color and texture, and signifying a distinctive style. Water features, furniture, decorative accessories, and lighting build on this theme, making spaces not only more functional but also more comfortable, personal, and inviting.

Decorative elements can be chosen to match indoor décor, creating a sense of unity and flow between interior and exterior spaces. Or they may be selected to create an entirely different kind of space that distinctly separates it from the house. Many homeowners prefer to tie outdoor spaces to the garden, emphasizing natural materials in their choice of furnishings, water features, and decorative accents. The great thing about designing an outdoor room is that the sky is your limit. As long as furnishings can weather the elements, just about anything goes.

◀ MEXICAN TILE AND ARIZONA FLAGSTONE enrich this colorful southwestern courtyard, with both the tile colors and flagstone echoed in the table and chair cushions. The fountain masks neighborhood noise, adding to the serene setting.

▶ GATES THAT CAN BE LOOKED THROUGH define boundaries yet encourage passersby to slow down and take a peak inside. The spindles on this handcrafted copper gate have been designed in the form of cattails, appropriately calling attention to the water garden just inside the courtyard.

▼ AN OPEN GATE is a sign of welcome. This one, with its bright yellow paint and widely spaced pickets, is especially cheerful and inviting. The straw hat adds a personal touch—expressing a warm and friendly invitation.

◄ LANDSCAPE STRUCTURES SUCH AS FENCES and gates play a strong role in setting the style and atmosphere of outdoor living spaces. This painted fence with playful cutouts creates a casual, lighthearted tone for activities that take place in this backyard.

▼ AN OUTDOOR ROOM with one or two carefully chosen objects can make a stronger statement than an outdoor room filled with decorative items. Here, the simplicity of paving materials and plantings allows the sculpture to shine and the distinctive arbor to define boundaries while maintaining an open feel.

Water Features

▼ THIS CARVED-STONE CONTAINER fills with water from the bamboo spout and then overflows into a basin located beneath the washed river stones. From there, a submersible pump recycles the water back through the bamboo spout. Hiding the bamboo in the foliage adds to the water feature's intrigue.

WATER IS MESMERIZING. It gives life to landscapes and outdoor living spaces and draws a crowd like a magnet. Whether a fish pond reflecting the autumn sky, the soft gurgling of a bubbling urn on a patio, or the energizing splash of a spa cascading into a swimming pool, water does more to create atmosphere in an outdoor room than perhaps any other element. It also has the unique ability to mask neighborhood noise.

Water features can be a significant component in an overall landscape plan or an easy addition to any deck, patio, porch, or garden. Ponds and waterfalls may require some basic construction skills, but it takes little more than a few inexpensive supplies and a couple of hours to create a container water garden or tabletop fountain. Many water features even come ready-made—just fill them with water and plug them into the nearest electrical outlet.

▲ THIS DECK FEELS MORE LIKE A DOCK because it overhangs the pond—which also gives the impression that the pond is larger than it really is. A pump was used to carry water to the dramatic cascade that spills over the wall, creating a special focal point.

◄ A CERAMIC BOWL, not to mention the birds of paradise plants, attracts feathered friends as well as the attention of passersby. The bowl also adds a sculptural element to the garden, and the crisp blue color complements nearby flowers.

▼ IT'S NOT EXACTLY a tabletop water feature, but water does flow into this striking stone table, which offers seating for six or more and is built into a retaining wall. Bottles of wine are often placed in the center of the table, where they are kept chilled by the water.

▲ A STEEP CITY LOT features a sunken courtyard outside a lower-level master bedroom. To bring the space to life, the hillside was terraced and planted, and a tiered waterfall of urns laid on their side was added to create a soothing, unique setting.

▶ THIS MANMADE, recirculating waterfall looks like a natural part of the landscape because it features a single type of stone, carries an appropriate amount of water, discreetly hides the water source, and is softened along the edges by lush plantings.

◄ THE SOUND OF TRICKLING WATER, along with a hollow knocking (when the bamboo fills with water and tips over), emanates from this Japanese "deer scarer," or *Shishi-Odoshi*. Although once used to scare wild animals from rice patties, they more commonly appear in ornamental gardens today.

Musical Waterworks

DRIP, SPLASH, SLOSH, GURGLE, TRICKLE—just think of all the words used to describe the sound of water. Armed with a basic understanding of how water makes sound, plus a little trial and error, it's possible to create a symphony of sounds with water features.

To achieve the desired tone, try adjusting the volume of water, the distance that it falls, and the surface over which it falls. A rule of thumb: The greater the volume of water and the greater the distance it falls, the louder the sound it makes. Whether the water tumbles over a rough surface or falls directly into a pool of water also changes its character. Of course, sometimes it's the serenity of still water we cherish the most.

◄ A BUBBLING URN adds sound, movement, and a vertical accent to this round fishpond. The plants soften the hard surfaces, tie the water feature into the surrounding garden, and provide shade for the fish.

► THIS BUBBLING FOUNTAIN is self-contained in a stone basin. By stacking the stones, this water feature, along with the striking ornamental grass, adds an upright element to a narrow lot, making it feel more spacious. Landscape lighting helps it make a dramatic statement at night.

▲ SIMPLE YET ELEGANT, this wall fountain features a cast-concrete raven waterspout and copper basin. Water flows from the basin to the fountain through one copper pipe; the other pipe hides the electrical cord, which runs to a small pump.

► SIMPLE STONE BASINS—or deceptively realistic, faux-stone basins, as shown here—make excellent birdbaths and are especially suitable for a naturalistic setting. This one is surrounded by blue star creeper and serves as a surprise element in a flagstone patio.

Taking Cues from Nature

WHEN PLACING NATURALISTIC WATER FEATURES in the landscape, it's helpful to glean ideas and inspiration from the natural world. Ponds, for instance, should be situated in a low area rather than atop a hill. And the edge of naturalistic ponds should be irregular and ideally edged with a combination of half-buried stone and natural plantings that run beyond the water's edge and into the water. Waterfalls and cascades require high vantage points in a landscape so that the water has someplace to fall. Streams should meander, not run in straight lines.

Contradicting these basic principles results in a nature-inspired water feature with an unnatural appearance.

Formal and contemporary water features, however, offer considerably more freedom when it comes to design and placement. Fountains and reflecting pools can be placed in courtyards, on patios, on a lawn, or in the garden. Small water features, such as bowls and basins, bubbling stones and urns, or container water gardens, can be tucked almost anywhere in a landscape.

▲ WATER LILIES ARE JUST BEGINNING to put on their summer show in this man-made, but naturalistic, pond. Other plants, which add contrasting textures and shapes to the water garden, include water lettuce, iris, water hyacinth, cannas, and sedges.

► THE WINDING COURSE and varied ledge heights of this man-made water feature make it look natural. The stream gently drops into a small pool, where a pump carries water back up to a carefully hidden stream head.

▼ EVEN IN WINTER, before the perennials have filled in, this bubbling granite stone draws the homeowner outdoors. It provides year-round structure in the garden and is enhanced by the surrounding tile work, which leads visually to the fountain as a central point in the courtyard.

◄ ANY CONTAINER THAT HOLDS WATER can be used to create a water garden. This large ceramic pot was placed in the garden to hold water lilies. Because the pot has a dark interior, it reflects its surroundings—in this case, colorful foliage plants.

▲ RAISED FISHPONDS can be built on a patio with materials that either match or contrast with the paving surface. By matching the brick, this pond blends in subtly with its surroundings, helping to create a soothing environment.

◄ FOUNTAINS COME IN ALL shapes and sizes. Some, like this copper frog, even provide a touch of whimsy. This fountain was placed in a shallow pool and connected to an inexpensive, submersible pump that runs on 110 voltage.

◄ AN ELEGANT TIERED FOUNTAIN like this one can be made at home. You just need a series of pedestals and basins, a small pump, and a pool into which the water can collect before recirculating. This one spills into a channel built into the deck.

▼ THE STACKED STONE NOT ONLY FRAMES the cast-stone wall fountain, but also conceals the pipe that carries water from the basin to the spout. Although the pipes could have been run behind the stucco wall, they would have been exposed in the neighbor's yard.

▲ THIS MOSS-COVERED STATUARY FOUNTAIN looks as if it has been around for years but it's new. To speed up the aging process of new statuary, spray the basin with a mixture of water and buttermilk, then rub some moss over the surface. The spores should germinate quickly.

Easy, Affordable Water Features

ANY CONTAINER THAT HOLDS WATER is fair game for a water feature. Simple or decorative birdbaths can anchor a border. Bowls, basins, pots, troughs, and barrels can be filled with water, moisture-loving plants (perched on bricks), and a few goldfish.

Water features of all sizes can benefit from the addition of a small fountain that runs on a fist-sized, submersible pump. Freestanding or tabletop fountains simply need to be filled with water and plugged into a nearby outlet. Just be sure that plugs and cords are designed for outdoor use and that outlets are covered and GFCI rated for safety.

Fashionable Outdoor Furniture

OUTDOOR FURNITURE HAS COME A LONG WAY from the plastic lawn chairs of old. As exterior furnishings have become an increasingly hot commodity, manufacturers have developed an impressive array of new materials and styles in price ranges to suit any budget.

While the climate and your personal tastes figure into the decision-making process, understanding how a space will be used—whether for dining, conversation, or sunning—is the most important factor. It's also important to know how many people will likely gather at a time. A cozy bistro table may suit a romantic dinner for two, but an extension table with folding chairs offers flexibility for larger groups.

Portability is also a plus outdoors. Medium-weight furniture can be easily rearranged into varied conversation groupings to suit different gatherings. Where harsh weather necessitates moving furniture indoors for winter, lighter-weight chairs that can be folded or stacked make the job much easier.

◄ COLORFUL SEAT CUSHIONS both soften these wrought-iron chairs (physically and visually) and color coordinate with the asters and purple fountain grass in the surrounding garden. The dark, airy wrought iron recedes visually, allowing the garden to remain center stage.

◄ WICKER HAS LONG BEEN USED outdoors, but the new faux-wicker, which is made from woven resin on a powder-coated steel base, wears much better and lasts much longer, resisting water, ultraviolet rays, mold, mildew, stains, and sagging.

▲ THIS UNIQUE, HANDCRAFTED WOODEN BENCH is right at home in the arid, southwestern landscape. Despite its intricate paint job, it's safe from the sun and infrequent showers thanks to the adequate shelter of the portico. The same is true for the handwoven rug.

► THIS ONE-OF-A-KIND BENCH was placed beneath an aging apple tree not so much as a place to sit but as a way to convey a sense of serenity. It marks the entrance to a fragrant garden, where visitors are encouraged to stroll about slowly and deliberately.

▲ WHY CHOOSE PLAIN CHAIRS when there are so many decorative styles to pick from? These Adirondack-style chairs are given a tropical twist with their palm-tree cutouts. Painted to match the shutters and flooring, they lend a sense of unity to this front porch.

▲ USING THE LAWN instead of a more formal patio or deck for this seating area produces an inviting, naturalistic aesthetic; the tall plantings offer an organic wall, creating a sense of privacy. The log-cabin-style chairs and well-worn table are light enough to be easily moved when it's time to cut the grass.

Weather-Worthy Fabrics

STANDARD UPHOLSTERY CUSHIONS AND FABRICS don't wear well outdoors. Outdoor cushions must be quick drying and mildew resistant. Likewise, fabrics should be quick drying and treated for UV, mildew, and stain resistance. The most common outdoor fabrics are solution-dyed acrylic and vinyl-encapsulated mesh. Both come in a wide range of colors and patterns for easy styling and color coordination.

For longevity, store cushions indoors during winter, spot-cleaning fabrics with mild soap and warm water. To remove mildew, spray on a solution of 1 cup bleach, 2 cups mild detergent, and 1 gallon of water. Allow the solution to soak in, then rinse thoroughly. For tough stains, use a fabric stain remover.

▲ OUTDOOR FURNITURE STYLES are just as distinctive as their indoor cousins. The only difference is that outdoor furniture must withstand harsh weather and more casual treatment. The curved profile, deep cushions, and glossy, protective finish of these pieces suit the formality of the architecture.

► THESE CLASSIC FRONT-PORCH ROCKERS are a southern favorite. Although few rockers are weather resistant, they are ideally suited to covered areas such as porches and sunrooms. Choose from natural, stained, and painted finishes with wooden or woven seats.

▼ SOME FURNITURE WORKS INDOORS AND OUT, such as this painted-metal and ceramic bistro table and chairs. It would look equally at home in a kitchen, sunroom, porch, or patio. An occasional sanding and a fresh coat of paint will keep it looking great for years.

◄ A SUMPTUOUS, ELEGANT SOFA like this one offers a stylish alternative to deck chairs, and its bright color makes a dramatic statement against the landscape. Just make sure any outdoor sofas feature quick-drying cushions designed to resist water, fading, mildew, and stains.

Wear and Care of Outdoor Furniture

SEASONAL CARE GREATLY EXTENDS the life-span of outdoor furniture. At least once a year, clean wood furniture with trisodium phosphate (TSP). Teak and cedar can weather naturally, but other woods need a fresh coat of varnish, stain, or paint.

Wash metal furniture with mild soap and warm water, and apply paste wax to prevent corrosion. Also rinse resin and plastic furniture. If stained or mildewed, wash with 1 cup of bleach, 2 cups of detergent, and 1 gallon of water. Gently machine-wash and hang-dry fabric seats, placing them on their frames while still damp to prevent shrinking. Vacuum outdoor wicker, then clean it with soapy water and apply a protective paste wax finish.

▲ THOSE WITH A KNACK for building things can make their own patio furniture. This stylized version of an Adirondack chair is a perfect example of great-looking, handcrafted furniture. A matching chest, which holds seat cushions but also works as an occasional table, stands nearby.

◀ THIS ARBOR PROVIDES a hanging structure for the hammock, as well as affording partial shade—a more comfortable arrangement in strong summer sun. It was tucked along one side of the backyard where young children playing on the lawn could be easily watched.

▲ TEAK IS A CLASSIC IN THE GARDEN. It adapts to many design styles, such as the contemporary set shown here, is sturdy and long lasting, and weathers to a beautiful gray patina with little or no care. It can even be left outdoors in winter (although it will last longer if stored indoors).

▶ IN ADDITION TO PROVIDING CASUAL SEATING, these wooden benches have been positioned along the edge of a low deck to define the boundaries of an outdoor room. Clusters of container plantings help to visually unite the sitting area with the surrounding garden.

◄ MIXING AND MATCHING OUTDOOR FURNITURE can form a sophisticated design style, just as it does indoors. In addition to wrought-iron and teak furniture, this outdoor room features both cushioned and noncushioned seating. It's just enough variety to make the space interesting without appearing busy.

► YARD SALES AND FLEA MARKETS are excellent sources for one-of-a-kind, mix-and-match furnishings. Old pieces in rough condition can be rescued and given new life, as was done with the old-fashioned folding chair shown here, with sandpaper, a fresh coat of paint, and a little creativity.

Simplify for a Soothing Setting

WHEN IT COMES TO OUTDOOR DÉCOR, **just about anything goes. But keep in mind that instead of being** framed by flat walls, floors, and ceilings, most outdoor rooms feature few flat surfaces and may be dominated by plant foliage, fences, arbors, detailed paving materials, and an ever-changing sky. So the surroundings are, visually speaking, busy to begin with.

If your goal is to create an energizing environment, go all out with bright colors and splashy designs. But if a soothing setting is preferred, keep the design simple. Limit the number of decorative objects in any one area, and select furnishings and accoutrements with natural finishes and clean lines. Also, limit the number of accent colors—whether in plantings or hard landscaping materials. Pastels, shades of white or gray, and harmonious (versus contrasting) colors tend to work best. And restricting the color palette to shades of green can be especially pleasing outdoors because it is such a natural choice.

▲ THIS SMALL DECK was designed as a getaway for one. The clean lines and natural materials of the teak chair, the gray walls, and the minimal decorative accents in the surroundings create a calm, soothing environment.

BUILT-IN SEATING

▶ A RUGGED BENCH is also a retaining wall. Because it's made from large stones and small boulders, it blends in unobtrusively with the surrounding landscape and provides a quiet spot to sit and enjoy the nearby pond.

▲ THIS PATIO FEATURES a mix of built-in and freestanding furnishings—all brightly colored to evoke a tropical theme emphasized by the plantings of palms, cannas, glory bush, and agapanthus. The tabletop lanterns add an appropriate finishing touch, with their blue panes picking up the color of nearby planters.

▲ THE FREESTANDING BENCH AND TABLE on this rooftop were designed to look like built-in furniture and make the most of limited space. They are solidly built—a significant consideration for rooftop locations where strong winds can be a challenge.

◄ ALTHOUGH THIS MAY NOT BE the most comfortable chair in the garden, it is the most unusual. Made entirely from recycled concrete, it offers a point of conversation if not a place to pause briefly while touring or working in the garden.

Accents and Accessories

STRUCTURES MAY DEFINE AN OUTDOOR SPACE and even signify its overall style, but accents and accessories give it personality. Such elements are limited only by your imagination and their ability to weather outdoor conditions. Objects can be mounted on house and garden walls, positioned in borders as focal points, clustered on tables or the ground, or hung from tree limbs and arbors.

With or without plants, containers are the most obvious choice for outdoor accents. Statuary and sculpture are also favorites, while weather-resistant pillows can add color and comfort to an outdoor room. Curtains and blinds create visual warmth while keeping inclement weather at bay, and market umbrellas and awnings do double duty as practical yet aesthetic enhancements. Even waterproof rugs are now available to help make patios look and feel more like rooms designed expressly for living. As long as the accessories express your style and complement their surroundings, you can't go wrong.

▲ MOSAICS, WHICH ARE CREATED BY PRESSING broken tiles and china into just-poured concrete, are easy to make and add a touch of color to any landscape. Here, bits and pieces of broken china and tile were transformed into a unique birdbath.

◄ DECORATIVE OBJECTS, especially when combined with architectural elements, can effectively carry out a decorating theme. Here, everything has an Asian flair—from the evergreen plantings and bamboo fence to the lantern and wall-mounted fish carving.

▲ FINDING NEW USES for common objects adds an element of surprise to any outdoor setting. This old garden bench has been put into service as a coffee table. Its faded paint echoes the colors in the pillows and flowers.

▲ THIS PORTICO USES A MIDDLE-EASTERN MOTIF to create a dramatic room without breaking the bank. The furnishings can easily be found at garage sales and discount stores and then dressed up with colorful fabrics. The hanging lantern, stars, and birdcage offer rich detail without a big price tag.

◄ MIRRORS ARE AN UNEXPECTED ELEMENT in outdoor rooms, but they can be used effectively to reflect light into shaded spaces and make a small space feel larger—just like indoors. These are flanked by curtains made from shade cloth, which is used to protect tender plants.

◄ IT'S A SNAP TO ADD A TOUCH of country charm, even in an urban setting. This homeowner transformed a small outdoor area with a faded board fence, old garden tools, a rustic bench, pots of ivy, casual paving, and ruffled pillows.

Art in the Garden

A RT TAKES MANY FORMS IN THE GARDEN—sculpture, statuary, found objects, architectural accents, folk art, and even mobiles. All help define the personality of an outdoor room or landscape and can bring a space to life. The key to using art successfully rests in its placement. Employ a favorite piece as a focal point at the end of a straight path or as a surprise element along a curving one, against a fence that can be viewed from indoors, as an anchor for a perennial border, or hanging from an arbor as an unexpected overhead object.

Landscapes are also excellent places to showcase collections of art. Try clustering several pieces to create a vignette, space them with a sense of rhythm to draw you through a garden, or showcase a single dominant piece within each visual space or outdoor room. This gives the art a sense of purpose and helps to avoid a haphazard, cluttered look that could detract from a collection's beauty.

Just make sure elements chosen as outdoor art can handle the elements. Porous objects may crack with winter's freeze-thaw cycle, metals may rust, some ceramic glazes may flake or fade from sun exposure, and wood may rot, especially if it's in contact with the ground.

▲ USING FAMILIAR OBJECTS In unfamiliar ways creates drama. Gazing globes are usually placed singly in the garden, atop a metal stand. Here, a whole row of gazing globes placed on the ground provides an unexpected counterpoint to the stark, yet dramatic, tree trunks.

CONTAINER PLANTINGS

◀ THIS GATHERING OF POTS makes a strong impression because the pots are staged on different levels. In addition to using a tiered plant stand, pots can be placed on steps, upturned empty pots, bricks, or outdoor furniture.

▼ PATHS, PATIOS, DECKS, AND PORCHES are excellent places to group container plantings. Cluster them along curves, at corners, next to posts, or adjacent to steps. This backyard arrangement exemplifies the visual interest that is created when the size of the clusters are varied.

▲ THESE CONTAINERS WERE PLANTED individually and clustered to create a striking grouping. They work well together because the succulents contrast in texture, shape, size, and color. If plants that looked similar had been chosen, the composition would have been much less interesting.

Quench Container Thirst

THE GREATEST CHALLENGE WITH GROWING PLANTS in pots is keeping them watered. It's not unusual for them to need water twice a day in hot, dry weather. To minimize watering needs, start with large pots. They hold more soil and won't dry out as quickly as small pots. Mix 2 parts potting soil with 1 part compost to improve water retention. Water-absorbing crystals, used modestly, can also help.

And finally, connect pots to a drip irrigation system with an automatic timer, especially if there are lots of pots in a concentrated area such as a deck or patio. That way, plants get watered even when you go on vacation.

▲ MATCHING CONTAINER PLANTINGS can be used to call attention to passageways—a door to the house, steps onto a deck, an arbor, or a path that leads around the side of a house. These planters filled with ferns mark the entrance to a garden path.

◄ THIS COLORFUL WINDOW BOX, which has been filled with easy-to-grow annuals, can be enjoyed from indoors and out. By using annuals, the planting can be changed several times during the year to keep it looking fresh and to reflect the changing seasons.

▼ BY PLACING MULTIPLE PLANTS in a single large pot, a self-contained garden is formed for this poolside patio. This planting works particularly well because it combines both upright and trailing plants. Within a matter of weeks, the sprawling petunias will obscure the planter altogether.

▲ CONTAINER PLANTINGS CREATE THE ILLUSION of walls around this small backyard patio, while a driftwood container hosts a living sculpture against the house wall and a tall container filled with trailing greenery softens the house corner. Together, they make a cozy setting for outdoor dining.

◄ WINDOW BOXES CAN BE HUNG on the walls of porches, decks, and patios to create focal points; this one is positioned near the front door where it makes a dramatic statement. Foliage plants were used to add a splash of color.

Landscape Lighting

TWO TYPES OF LIGHTING ARE ESSENTIAL in an outdoor room: functional and accent. Functional lighting—such as downlights mounted in trees or along a house eave, lanterns mounted on a wall, chandeliers hanging from tree limbs or arbors, and path lights placed around a patio or path—make it easy to move about safely, cook dinner on the grill, and see what you're eating for dinner.

Accent lighting creates ambience in outdoor rooms and can also be used to highlight architectural features of a home and garden. It may be a spotlight on a sculpture, uplights in trees, string lights across an awning, or candlelight on a table. The secret to successful outdoor lighting is to provide just enough light, creating a subtle effect rather than an overwhelming one.

▼ THE STRING LIGHTS DRAPED AROUND this rustic gazebo add a festive note to any gathering in the backyard. String lights can also be wrapped around tree limbs, strung across an arbor or porch eave, or hung around an umbrella.

▼ THE DROPPED CEILING in this outdoor pavilion permits the use of strategically placed can lights that can be adjusted with a dimmer. Courtyard lights are kept to a minimum and used primarily to move about safely, which allows the pavilion to remain the focal point.

▲ OUTDOOR FIXTURES CAN BE as beautiful as those intended for indoor use. This custom-designed Craftsman-style lantern was placed above a retaining wall where it helps illuminate a small patio. It is located just below eye level, so the cap deflects any potential glare.

▲ TIKI TORCHES ARE STILL POPULAR, but now there are many more styles of torches to choose from. These attractive copper fixtures hold candles rather than lamp oil. The glass windows improve safety and keep wind from blowing the flames out.

▲ THESE CANDLELIT LANTERNS are positioned to draw you along the path toward an undisclosed but intriguing destination. Lanterns are an affordable and highly effective way to light certain outdoor spaces but may not put out enough light for tasks like cooking.

◄ SPAS AND POOLS emit an inviting glow when illuminated from within. This spa features several incandescent lights encased in a watertight shell. Fiber-optic lighting can also be used underwater and is often run in a strip around the edge of a pool.

Designing a Lighting Scheme

OUTDOOR LIGHTING SCHEMES can be as simple or complex as needed. The most flexible plans are those designed in zones, much like modern kitchen lighting. Overhead lighting on one switch, path lighting on another, and accent lighting on a third is practical and energy efficient.

Also, keep in mind that several low-output lights produce a more pleasing effect than a single high-output light; think of the difference between a single bright ceiling light and several lower wattage table lamps in a living room. It's not just a matter of being able to see, it's about creating atmosphere and feeling comfortable outdoors. For best results, discuss specific lighting needs with a professional lighting designer.

▲ THIS GAZEBO AND NEIGHBORING TREE are dramatically lit by uplights that are anchored in the ground to make them the focal point of the backyard. Highly focused downlights, placed in nearby trees, illuminate the path to the gazebo without casting light on the lawn.

▼ ALTHOUGH THESE CRAFTSMAN-STYLE path lanterns glow like candlelight, they are actually tinted shades hiding bulbs powered by a low-voltage electric current. Even do-it-yourself kits now come with elegant decorative fixtures like these and are perfect for small-scale installations.

Light of the Party

OOD FOOD, GOOD FRIENDS, GOOD MUSIC. And, of course, don't forget the importance of good lighting. Whether you need supplemental lighting for an extra large gathering or just want to create great atmosphere, a few lighting enhancements can help make any party a smashing success.

Flickering torches can be placed around a patio, pool deck, or lawn. String lights can be wrapped around trees and shrubs, along porch railings, or across awnings and arbors. And candles placed in sand-filled bags or metal cans featuring decorative cutouts can be used to light the way from parking areas to the party. Sturdy candles set on bases or enclosed in lanterns can be placed on tables and any other flat surfaces. And finally, consider hanging lanterns from tree limbs for soft overhead lighting. Both electric and enclosed candlelight models are available to suit your sense of style.

▲ AMONG THE NEWEST LIGHTS on the market are all-weather table and floor lamps. Although some are plugged into outdoor electrical outlets, this one comes with a rechargeable battery, eliminating electrical cords that might get in the way in many outdoor locations.

▲ PUNCHED-TIN CANDLEHOLDERS add a whimsical folk-art touch to a backyard patio. They are inexpensive and easy to make. In fact, they would make a great afternoon project for a couple of creative teenagers with cans, paint, a hammer, and nails.

▲ PAPER LANTERNS EMIT A SOFT GLOW and can be easily hung from trees, arbors, or pergolas. Several paper lanterns, perhaps with different color shades, can be hung at varying heights as if they were mobiles hanging from a ceiling.

Outdoor Recreation

OUTDOOR RECREATION HAS ADVANCED SIGNIFICANTLY in the last couple of decades, evolving from tire swings and sprinklers to elaborate play structures, game courts, and virtual water parks And it's not just the kids who have benefited; adults are getting in on the action and discovering a more invigorating version of family time. Whether it's your dream to gather around a pool or turn your backyard into a back nine, options abound for every whim.

Since backyard recreation is now for kids of all ages, it's important to include something for each member of the family. Begin by providing safe play spaces for young children that can be easily viewed from indoors. Older children still need to be within earshot, but they appreciate a bit more privacy, perhaps a tree house or game court located farther from the house. Teens often enjoy group activities—anything from roller hockey and skateboarding to soccer and basketball—or they may need a place to practice their jump shots and pitching for the school team.

Adults tend to combine recreation and entertaining, so place putting greens, croquet courts, or an outdoor pool table near the patio. And, of course, friends and family will enjoy spending time around a pool—whether it's swimming laps, playing water volleyball, or just soaking up the sun.

◀ A VARIETY OF GATHERING PLACES makes this swimming pool a favorite destination any time of day. The broad pool deck is ideal for sunning or entertaining, the arbor casts shade over a dining area, and the pool house provides shelter from wind or sudden rain showers.

Kids' Play Spaces

UNDER THE RIGHT CONDITIONS, CHILDREN CAN ENTERTAIN THEMSELVES for hours. It helps to provide a variety of play spaces, as the interests of young minds can shift quickly. A lawn (it doesn't have to be large) for running around, kicking balls, and playing games is essential. A play structure with mix-and-match elements for climbing, sliding, and swinging can provide years of enjoyment and help improve coordination. A fort, playhouse, or tree house offers a fun, safe place in which to escape and engage the imagination. And kid-sized tables and chairs are ideal for quiet activities such as board games, tea parties, and art projects. All play areas benefit from a soft, cushioning layer of mulch or sand—especially around play structures or rough-and-tumble play spaces.

▼ CAREFUL ATTENTION TO LANDSCAPING makes this backyard a desirable destination for kids and adults alike. A play structure and small lawn are tucked neatly alongside a garden, while a curving path doubles as garden access and a tricycle path.

▲ KIDS NEED A PLACE TO UNWIND after rough-and-tumble activities, engage in quiet games, munch on afternoon snacks, or simply visit with friends. This colorfully shaded kids-size picnic table fits the bill perfectly as a space kids can call their own.

◄ SANDBOXES ARE FAVORITE play spaces for young children. This one was built from wood with a flat edge for seating and filled with play sand—a fine-grain sand that (unlike coarse builders' sand) has been filtered and cleaned and will not stain clothing.

► SIMULATED ROCK-CLIMBING WALLS are not limited to outdoor adventure stores. Children love the experience, so a low climbing wall with strong, closely placed hand- and footholds is ideal for backyard playgrounds. This one is approximately 4 ft. high and sits atop a soft pad of mulch.

▲ A CHALLENGING SITE doesn't have to limit activities. This custom-designed play structure takes advantage of a steeply sloping lot that has been terraced for improved accessibility. A slide from the sheltered lookout tower makes it easy for kids to reach the lower level.

◄ THERE ARE SEVERAL WAYS to go from the lower terrace back to the upper level. Children enjoy climbing this ladder or rescaling the slide, but parents tend to prefer steps, which are built at either end of the terrace.

Exploring Nature with Children

BACKYARDS ARE THE PERFECT PLACE for children to learn about nature, whether through gardening or by creating a wildlife habitat for birds, toads, and butterflies.

Small gardens featuring giant flowers, easy-to-grow edibles, fuzzy foliage, and plants that attract butterflies can be planted and tended by children. For added interest, consider the following kid-friendly ideas: Grow beans up poles to form a teepee; create a corn or sunflower house by planting in a square and leaving a gap for the door; train a row of willow twigs into a living tunnel.

Pint-sized gardening tools are available to help with the task, and kids can have fun creating their own scarecrows each season. Older children may enjoy building a small greenhouse from salvaged supplies.

Backyard habitats provide food, water, cover, and safe places for small wildlife to raise their young. Trees and shrubs with nuts and fruit, as well as annuals and perennials with edible seed heads or nectar, will attract birds and butterflies. Shallow ponds are ideal for goldfish and for attracting toads. Birds will flock to birdfeeders, birdbaths, and birdhouses in any backyard. Even butterfly houses, bat houses, and toad houses will be occupied by guests in due time.

Bean teepee

Make wider and with a small opening for kids to crawl through. Use approximately eight poles, each 9 ft. to 12 ft. tall.

"Doorway"

Willow tunnel

Sunflower house

▲ KIDS LOVE TO PLAY this handyman's version of a musical instrument, which is located beneath a tree house. Long bolts with oversized nuts were mounted on a swivel so that they could be used to strike the hollow copper pipes of varying lengths.

▶ A THICK, CUSHIONING LAYER of mulch provides a soft landing surface beneath this homemade backyard play structure, which features a fort, swings, tire swing, hammock, and slide. At least 6 in. to 8 in. of mulch is essential; some experts recommend 10 in. to 12 in.

▲ MUCH OF THE PLAYGROUND EQUIPMENT sold today is available in modular units, making it adaptable for varied budgets and kids of different ages. This one features a variety of climbing, sliding, swinging, and sitting elements to encourage a combination of quiet, athletic, and adventurous activities.

◄ IT'S NOT EXACTLY A TREE HOUSE, but the tree makes going down this slide more exciting and is a space-saving solution in a small backyard. The slide is attached to a small wooden platform for support and can be easily removed when the children outgrow it.

▲ TREE HOUSES CAN BE BUILT in a tree, around a tree, between trees, or on posts. This one is perched atop three sturdy limbs and features board-and-batten construction with a shingled, gable roof. The colorful paint job adds a sense of whimsy.

◄ THINGS ARE SLIGHTLY ASKEW in this brightly painted storybook playhouse. Surrounded by large-leaved hollyhocks and a flower-filled window box, it is a safe, convenient, and inviting play space that sparks the imagination of young children.

▲ A FEW OUNCES OF CREATIVITY can transform a garden shed into a magical playhouse. Painted shutters, window boxes, foundation plantings, and a faux chimney make this pint-sized place look like home. Tucked into a corner of the property, it doesn't overwhelm the backyard.

Creative Play Spaces

PLAY STRUCTURES DON'T HAVE TO BREAK THE BUDGET. A little imagination goes a long way when it comes to creative play spaces for young minds. Build a small platform for an outdoor stage or construct a puppet theater from plywood. Design an obstacle course that requires climbing a small tree, scrambling over a log, crawling beneath a hedge, and jumping over a puddle. Hang a tire swing from a strong tree limb with heavy gauge rope. Pitch a tent for backyard sleepovers. Keep chalk handy for drawing on sidewalks or a recycled slate slab. Get your kids involved in coming up with ideas for the added benefit of sharpening creative thinking skills.

◄ BEING IN THE TREETOPS changes the way in which the world is viewed—both literally and figuratively speaking. This open-air deck offers kids a squirrel's-eye view of the backyard, while the garden swing gives parents or care-givers a place to relax nearby.

▼ THIS SCALED-DOWN VERSION of a shed is just the right size to lure young children down the garden path. By positioning it in the midst of a garden, children are afforded a unique oppor-tunity to observe and interact with nature.

▲ THIS UNIQUE TIRE SWING offers a new twist on an old theme. Strips of recycled tire rubber were ingeniously reassembled to create a swinging horse and then hung from a sturdy limb with heavy-duty rope.

▲ UPSTAIRS, DOWNSTAIRS, AND UP on the roof—this custom-built tree house (actually built on sturdy posts) offers a variety of indoor and outdoor places for keeping an eye on the neighborhood or escaping for a little privacy.

Game Areas

GAMES AREN'T JUST FOR THE YOUNG. They're also for the young at heart. In fact, they are a great way for families to spend more time together, as structured activities will often interest even the most independent teenagers. A small lawn planted with a tough turf grass is ideal for tag, croquet, softball, or volleyball. Other sports—such as horseshoes, shuffleboard, bocce ball, tennis, and basketball—require courts. Modular, suspended flooring, which is safer on the joints than concrete or asphalt, is now available in various court sizes suitable for backyard installation. Practicing on a backyard putting green is a sure way to improve a golf handicap, while billiard and table tennis equipment now come in waterproof models that are ideal for patios and pool decks. Paved areas for skateboarding, rollerblading, and roller hockey are also increasing in popularity. And a comfortable table and chairs are perfect for playing cards and board games.

► MOST BACKYARD PUTTING GREENS are made from low-maintenance artificial turf and come in a range of sizes and shapes. This one has been beautifully landscaped with boulders, naturalistic plantings, and even a waterfall.

▼ DINING TABLES CAN DO double duty as game tables on a porch, patio, or deck. Located beneath the shelter of a screened porch, this one is ideal for sunny or rainy day activities. Games can be stored nearby in a chest or cabinet.

◄ THIS BOCCE COURT is an eye-catching gathering space in a formal landscape (especially when viewed through this granite sculpture). The court itself is sunken, edged in cut stone, and filled with crushed gravel. It is surrounded by a tree-lined avenue, along with cast stone benches.

▲ A RECTANGULAR AREA was carved out of this sloping backyard to create a flat game area. Although it is currently being used for croquet, it is also an appropriate shape and size for badminton, volleyball, and children's games like capture the flag.

▶ POOL TABLES ARE NOW AVAILABLE in waterproof out-door models. This pool table was placed on a sunken game terrace located between the house and a broader terrace used for dining and entertaining. It's a favorite spot for the family teenagers.

▼ DESIGNED MORE FOR CONTEMPLATION than recreation, mazes and labyrinths provide a walking meditation for adults. Children also find them mesmerizing. This labyrinth was created by laying paths flush with the lawn. Mazes—in which you can't see where you are—are designed with hedge-lined paths.

◄ TABLE TENNIS IS A GOOD SPORT for the patio or terrace. Although this game table is weather resistant, its useful life can be extended by folding it up and rolling it under a nearby eave when not in use or if wet weather is in the forecast.

Playing It Safe

BACKYARD GAMES ARE ONLY FUN if nobody gets hurt. Game lawns should be flat and free from obstructions. Lawns and courts—in fact, any play spaces—should be placed away from fireplaces, grills, outdoor furniture, hard landscape surfaces, and fragile plantings. Activities that involve balls are best played away from windows and outdoor cooking areas. Play sets and swings need a thick layer of bark mulch, recycled rubber mulch, or play sand beneath them to create a soft landing surface. Also be sure to provide adequate lighting, as evenings are a favorite time for outdoor games and activities.

▲ CHILDREN LOVE TO BOUNCE (and parents love the extra energy it burns off)! Adding protective netting along the edges of this trampoline improves its safety and gives the parents peace of mind. Even with safety netting, however, children should be supervised when playing on a trampoline.

▲ GENEROUS LAWNS ARE THE MOST versatile recreational spaces in any yard. For safety and enjoyment, they should be level and free of stones, tree roots, and holes. This one is used for a variety of activities, from croquet to touch football to games of tag.

► THIS SMALL LAWN is just large enough for a child's game of soccer. Tough turf grasses such as perennial ryegrass, tall fescue, and St. Augustine grass are essential for recreational lawns that get trampled by feet on a day-to-day basis.

◄ THE DRIVEWAY IS STILL the most popular place to locate a basketball goal, but this home court is unique because it features built-in benches along the sidelines. Also, because the goal is attached to an arbor, the ball will not get stuck on the roof.

▲ ALTHOUGH THIS OUTDOOR CHESS SET is more for show than recreation, guests at parties have been known to engage in a not-so-serious game using these life-sized players. Lighter-weight, oversized models—which are designed for play—are also commercially available.

◄ KAYAKING, CANOEING, PADDLE BOAT-ING, and rowing are excellent forms of exercise for those fortunate enough to live near the water. These boats have been pulled up on a permanent dock that has been built from rot-resistant ipé, a tropical hardwood, at the edge of the patio.

Swimming Pools

SWIMMING POOLS ARE MAKING A BIG SPLASH in backyard recreation, with new pool construction at an all-time high. That's because new construction technology has made installing a pool more affordable, and new features have made them more inviting. No longer just rectangular holes in the ground, pools come in just about any shape, size, and style—from long, narrow lap pools to multipurpose recreational pools to naturalistic swimming pools that look more like ponds. (Just keep in mind that you'll need to include a straight stretch if you plan to swim laps.)

Fountains, waterfalls, underwater benches with jets, beach-style entries, and wading areas make pools undeniably alluring and allow a pool's luxuries to be tailor-made to your liking. When designing a pool, it's important to think beyond the water, too. Design spaces for relaxing in sun or shade, and include areas for cooking, dining, and entertaining to make your pool area as versatile and user-friendly as possible.

▼ ALTHOUGH DESIGNED WITH NATURAL MATERIALS to complement the surrounding gardens, this pool is large enough for engaging in casual water sports and offers an uninterrupted area for swimming shortlaps. A broad deck along one side offers ample space for relaxing in the sun.

▲ THIS NATURALISTIC SWIMMING POOL and spa is edged in artificial boulders and features a tumbling waterfall. It is surrounded by plantings and a small patio rather than a broad pool deck, which helps it to blend in with the surrounding landscape.

◄ IN KEEPING WITH THE INDIGENOUS LANDSCAPE, these Connecticut home-owners edged their pool in mortared stone rather than in concrete. And since the pool is covered for much of the year, they positioned it so it wouldn't be viewed directly from the picture window in winter.

◄ IT'S ALWAYS A GOOD IDEA to include a shady area near a swimming pool for escaping the sun's rays. Even those who may prefer not to swim will appreciate having a shady spot in which to relax and feel a part of pool-side activities.

▼ SMALL SWIMMING POOLS such as this one are designed more for relaxation and recreation than for swimming laps. It features a gradual entry rather than steps and is highlighted by a recirculating waterfall and raised terrace, making it the focal point of a small, enclosed backyard.

▲ A BROAD TERRACE FLOWS EASILY from multiple rooms of the house to the expansive pool deck below. The brick on the pool deck complements the accent brick in the home and in the step risers to create a sense of continuity.

▲ MORE FORMAL OR TRADITIONAL HOMES are best complemented with conventional, geometrically designed pools. While this one is surrounded by a broad, cut-stone deck, the strategic placement of bold container plantings helps create intimate gathering spaces.

Site Pools in the Sun

THE SWIMMING SEASON CAN BE EXTENDED by placing a pool in full sun, where it will warm up earlier in spring and stay warm longer into the fall. A pool in full sunlight can also be enjoyed more hours during the day, and it is less likely to be littered by falling leaves or needles.

Although a pool should be positioned for maximum sun exposure, don't forget to include a shady spot nearby for cooling off on a hot day or escaping the sun's harsh rays. Arbors, gazebos, porches, porticos, and pool houses all serve this role well. Umbrellas and awnings are also excellent options for shade.

▶ DIVING BOARDS HAVE DECLINED in popularity due to growing safety concerns, but large jump rocks have taken their place. They don't provide spring, but they do still offer a place from which to jump safely into the deep end of a pool.

▼ THIS POOL DECK FEATURES FOUR separate seating areas—some in the sun and some in the shade of an arbor or umbrella to accommodate everybody's preference. The pool house provides a convenient location for changing clothes, storing pool furniture, and preparing casual meals.

▲ FOR SERIOUS SWIMMERS, a lap pool should be at least 45 ft. long—otherwise, more time is spent turning than swimming. This L-shaped lap pool features a painted lane line on the pool bottom and still accommodates general recreational activities in the broad end.

◄ THIS SLEEK AND CONTEMPORARY raised pool features a vanishing edge. A thin layer of water spills over the pool's edge into a basin below and is then recirculated back into the pool. When viewed from indoors, the pool water appears to merge with the lake in the distance.

Resources

Additional Reading

Architecture in the Garden by James Van Sweden. Random House, 2002.

Graphic Guide to Site Construction by Rob Thallon and Stan Jones. The Taunton Press, Inc., 2003.

Garden Masterclass by John Brookes. Dorling Kindersley, 2002.

Taunton's Backyard Idea Book by Lee Anne White. The Taunton Press, Inc., 2004.

Taunton's Deck and Patio Idea Book by Julie Stillman and Jane Gitlin. The Taunton Press, Inc., 2003.

Taunton's Pool Idea Book by Lee Anne White. The Taunton Press, Inc., 2004.

Better Homes and Gardens Outdoor Kitchens. Meredith Books, 2004.

Outdoor Rooms: Designs for Porches, Terraces, Decks, Gazebos by Julie D. Taylor. Rockport Publishers, 2001.

Garden & Patio Living Spaces. Sunset Books, 1999.

Building Barbecues & Outdoor Kitchens. Sunset Books, 2001.

Product Sources

All Pro Putting Greens
(800) 334-9005
www.allprogreens.com
(backyard putting greens)

BBQ.com
(877) 743-2269
www.bbq.com
(grills, beverage centers, hearths, lighting)

Bellacor
(877) 723-5522
www.bellacor.com
(furniture, lighting, décor)

Brookstone®
(866) 576-7337
www.brookstone.com
(furniture, lighting, décor, recreational products)

Casuali
www.casuali.com
(furniture, firepits)

Cedar Store
(888) 293-2339
www.cedarstore.com
(furniture)

ChildLife®
(800) 467-9464
www.childlife.com
(backyard play structures)

Comfort Channel
(800) 303-7574
www.comfortchannel.com
(outdoor kitchens, hearths, furnishings, recreation)

Dacor® Outdoor
(800) 793-0093
www.dacor.com
(grills, accessories)

DecKorators™
(800) 332-5724
www.deckorators.com
(wood and metal deck railings)

Detailed Play Systems
(800) 398-7565
www.detailedplay.com
(modular background play structures)

Fire Science, Inc.
(716) 568-2224
www.fire-science.com
(fireplaces, firepits, heaters, grills, torches)

Frontgate®
(888) 263-9850
www.frontgate.com
(outdoor living and home furnishings)

Gas Grill Guy
(800) 811-9890
www.gasgrillguy.com
(grills, grilling accessories, furniture)

G I Designs
(877) 442-6773
www.gidesigns.net
(copper garden structures, hearths, furniture, décor)

The Grill Outlet
(800) 657-6124
www.thegrilloutlet.com
(grills)

Hammacher Schlemmer
(800) 321-1484
www.hammacher.com
(furniture, lighting, grills, pest control, pool gear)

HomePortfolio®
www.homeportfolio.com
(search portfolio for furniture, lighting, spas, fountains)

Hot Tub Guide
www.hottubguide.com
(hot tubs, spas)

Lane®venture
(800) 235-3558
www.laneventure.com
(outdoor furniture, kitchens, fireplaces)

Living Tree, LLC
(610) 952-5209
www.livingtreeonline.com
(tree house design and construction)

Outdoor Kitchens Depot
(877) 743-2269
www.outdoorkitchensdepot.com
(outdoor kitchens, grills, hearths)

Patio Hearth
(877) 649-9800
www.patiohearth.com
(fireplaces, grills, mosquito control products)

Plow & Hearth®
(800) 494-7544
www.plowhearth.com
(furniture, accessories)

The Porch Company
(615) 662-2886
www.porchco.com
(custom porch design and
construction)

Putter's Edge
(800) 875-3151
www.putters-edge.com
(backyard putting greens)

Putting Greens Direct
(866) 743-4653
www.puttinggreens
direct.com
(backyard putting greens)

Rittenhouse
(877) 488-1914
www.rittenhouse.ca
(outdoor lamps, garden
tools, pest control
products)

Shady Lady Lighting
(800) 343-1954
www.shadyladylighting
.com
(outdoor lamps)

Smith & Hawken®
(800) 940-1170
www.smithandhawken
.com
(patio and garden
furnishings)

Sport Court®
International
(800) 421-8112
www.sportcourt.com
(backyard game courts)

Swing Sets Direct
(800) 264-9142
www.swingsetsdirect.com
(play structures, tire
swings, trampolines)

Thos. Baker
(877) 855-1900
www.thosbaker.com
(outdoor furniture)

Westminster Teak
(888) 592-8325
www.westminsterteak
.com
(furniture, umbrellas,
storage, accessories)

Organizations

The American Institute of
Architects
(202) 626-7300
www.aia.org

Association of
Professional Landscape
Designers
(717) 238-9780
www.apld.org

American Society of
Landscape Architects
(202) 898-2444
www.asla.org

Concrete Network
www.concretenetwork
.com

Hearth, Patio & Barbecue
Association
(703) 522-0086
www.hpba.org

Master Pools Guild
(800) 392-3044
www.masterpoolsguild
.com

National Association
of Home Builders
(800) 368-5242
www.nahb.org

National Gardening
Association
www.kidsgardening.com
(features a parents' primer
on gardening with kids)

National Kitchen & Bath
Association
(800) 843-6522
www.nkba.org

National Spa & Pool
Institute
(703) 838-0083
www.nspi.org

National Wildlife
Federation
www.nwf.org/backyard-
wildlifehabitat/
(information on creating a
backyard wildlife habitat)

Credits

p. ii–iii: Photo © Lee Anne White.

p. v: Photo © Tim Street-Porter.

p. vi–1: (left to right) Brian Vanden Brink, photo © 2005; © Deidra Walpole; © J. Paul Moore; © Allan Mandell; © 2005 Carolyn L. Bates/carolynbates.com.

p. 2: Photo © Allan Mandell.

p. 3: (top) Brian Vanden Brink, photo © 2005; (bottom left) © Lee Anne White; (bottom right) © Dency Kane.

CHAPTER 1

p. 4: Brian Vanden Brink, photo © 2005.

p. 5: Photo © Deidra Walpole.

p. 6: (top) Photo © Deidra Walpole; Design: Ruby Begonia Fine Gardens; (bottom) Photo © Lee Anne White; Design: Simmonds & Associates.

p. 7: Photo © Deidra Walpole; Design: Ruby Begonia Fine Gardens.

p. 8: Photos: © Lee Anne White; Designs: Desert Sage Builders.

p. 9: (top) Photo © Lee Anne White; Design: Linda Marr & Jackye Meinicke; (bottom) Photo © Deidra Walpole; Design: The Green Scene.

p. 10: Photo © Lee Anne White; Design: Four Dimensions Landscape.

p. 11: (left) Photo © Allan Mandell; Design: Milari Hare; (right) Photo © Lee Anne White; Design: Simmonds & Associates.

p. 12: (top) Photo © Lee Anne White; Design: JC Enterprise Services Inc.; (bottom) Photo © Lee Anne White.

p. 13: Photo courtesy Dacor.

p. 14: (top) Photo courtesy Dacor; (bottom) Photo

© Allan Mandell; Design: Ron Wagner & Nani Waddoups.

p. 15: (top) Photo courtesy DACOR; (center) Photo © Lee Anne White; (bottom) Photo © Lee Anne White; Design: Betty Romberg.

p. 16: Photo © Deidra Walpole; Design: The Green Scene.

p. 17: (left) Photo © Deidra Walpole; Design: Ruby Begonia Fine Gardens; (right) Photo © Lee Anne White; Design: Desert Sage Builders.

p. 18: (top) Photo © Deidra Walpole; Design: The Green Scene; (bottom) Photo © Deidra Walpole; Design: Mark David Levine Design Associates.

p. 19: Photo © Lee Anne White; Design: Colette Bullock.

p. 20: (top) Photo © Lee Anne White; Design: Michelle Derviss; (bottom) Photo © Lee Anne White; Design: Jim Harrington Garden Design.

p. 21: Photo © Lee Anne White; Design: Linda Marr and Jackye Meinicke.

p. 22: (left) Photo courtesy Paul Faaborg/topgrill.com; (right) Photo © Lee Anne White; Design: Desert Sage Builders.

p. 23: (top) Photo © Lee Anne White; Design: JC Enterprise Services, Inc.; (bottom) Photo © Lee Anne White; Design: Bill Feinberg, Allied Kitchen & Bath.

p. 24: Photo: Brian Vanden Brink, photo © 2005; Design: Polhemus Savery Da Silva.

p. 25: (top & bottom) Photos Brian Vanden Brink, photo © 2005; Design: Mark Hutker & Associates Architects.

p. 26: (left) Brian Vanden

Brink, photo © 2005; Design: Polhemus Savery Da Silva; (right) Photo © Allan Mandell; Design: Myrna Wright.

p. 27: (top) Photo © Tim Street-Porter; (bottom) Photo by Todd Meier, © The Taunton Press, Inc.; Design: Alan Franz.

p. 28: (left) Photo © Allan Mandell; Design: Linda Ernst; (top right) Photo © Lee Anne White; Design: JC Enterprise Services, Inc.; (bottom right) Photo © Lee Anne White; Design: Dan Cleveland.

p. 29: (top) Photo © Allan Mandell; Design: Pamela Burton; (bottom) Photo © Allan Mandell; Design: Les Bugajski.

p. 30: (left) Photo © Lee Anne White; Design: Four Dimensions; (right) Photo © Lee Anne White; Design: Michelle Derviss.

p. 31: (left) Photo © Allan Mandell; Design: Ron Wagner & Nani Waddoups; (right) Photo © Lee Anne White; Design: Richard McPherson.

p. 32: (top) Photo © Deidra Walpole; Design: Robert Marien; (bottom) Photo © Lee Anne White; Design: Colette Bullock.

p. 33: (left) Photo © Deidra Walpole; Design: Ruby Begonia Fine Gardens; (right) Photo © Deidra Walpole; Design: Flower to the People.

CHAPTER 2

p. 34: Photo © Deidra Walpole; Design: Van Atta Associates.

p. 35: Photo © Anne Gummerson Photography.

p. 36: Photo © Allan Mandell.

p. 37: (top) Brian Vanden

Brink, photo © 2005; (bottom) Photo © Lee Anne White; Design: Four Dimensions.

p. 38: (top) Photo © Lee Anne White; Design: Simmonds & Associates; (bottom) Photo by Charles Miller, © The Taunton Press, Inc.; Design: Roc Caivano.

p. 39: Photo © Allan Mandell; Design: Pamela Burton.

p. 40: (top) Photo © Allan Mandell; Design: Julie Moir Messervy; (bottom) Photo © Deidra Walpole; Design: Grossman Design Specialists.

p. 41: (top) Photo © Lee Anne White; Design: Simmonds & Associates; (bottom) Photo © 2005 Carolyn L. Bates/carolynbates.com.

p. 42: Brian Vanden Brink, photo © 2005.

p. 43: (left) Brian Vanden Brink, photo © 2005; Design: Quinn Evans Architects; (right) Brian Vanden Brink, photo © 2005.

p. 44: (top) Brian Vanden Brink, photo © 2005; Design: Sally Weston Architects; (bottom) Photo © Lee Anne White; Design: Joan Lewis & Nancy Caplan.

p. 45: Photo © Lee Anne White.

p. 46: Photo © Tria Giovan.

p. 47: (top) Photo © Tria Giovan; (bottom) Photo by Roe A. Osborn, © The Taunton Press, Inc.; Design: Jill Fuerstneau Sousa

p. 48: (left & right) Photos © Tria Giovan.

p. 49: (left) Photo © Tim Street-Porter; (right) Photo © Lee Anne White; Design: JC Enterprise Services, Inc.

p. 50: (top) Photo by Charles Bickford, © The Taunton Press, Inc.; Design by Sarah

Susanka, architect; (bottom) Photo © Lee Anne White, Design: Lynda Montgomery & Reflections of Nature.

p. 51: (top left & bottom) Photos © Tria Giovan; (top right) Photo © Jerry Pavia.

p. 52: Brian Vanden Brink, photo © 2005; Design: Elliott, Elliott, Norellus Architecture.

p. 53: (top) Brian Vanden Brink, photo © 2005; Design: Pete Bethanis, architect; (bottom) Brian Vanden Brink, photo © 2005; Design: Polhemus Savery Da Silva.

p. 54: (top) Photo © Deidra Walpole; Design: Mark David Levine Design Group; (bottom) Photo © Tria Giovan.

p. 55: (left) Photo © Lee Anne White; Design: Lee Anne White; (right) Photo © Allan Mandell; Design: Thomas Vetter.

p. 56: (top) Photo © Lee Anne White; Design: Simmonds & Associates; (bottom left) Photo © Tria Giovan; (bottom right) Photo © 2005 Carolyn L. Bates/carolynbates.com; Design: The Chushman Design Group, Inc.

p. 57: Photo © Deidra Walpole.

p. 58: Photo © Deidra Walpole.

p. 59: (top) Photo by Todd Meier, © The Taunton Press, Inc.; Design: James Woodel & Kimmey Tilley; (bottom) Photo © www.kenricephoto.com.

CHAPTER 3

p. 60: Photo © J. Paul Moore; Design: The Porch Company.

p. 61: Brian Vanden Brink, photo © 2005.

p. 62: Brian Vanden Brink,
photo © 2005; Design: Peter Breese.

p. 63: (top) Brian Vanden Brink, photo © 2005; Design: John Cole, architect; (bottom) Photo by Daniel S. Morrison, © The Taunton Press, Inc.; Design: Al Platt, architect.

p. 64: Photo © Tria Giovan.

p. 65: (left) Photo © J. Paul Moore; Design: The Porch Company; (right) Photo © Tria Giovan.

p. 66–67: Photos © J. Paul Moore; Designs: The Porch Company.

p. 68: (top) Photo © Tria Giovan; (bottom) Photo by Roe A. Osborn, © The Taunton Press, Inc.; Design: Paul DeGroot, architect.

p. 69: (top) Photo by Charles Bickford, © The Taunton Press, Inc.; Design: Sarah Susanka, architect; (bottom) Photo © Anne Gummerson Photography; Design: Hammond-Wilson Architects and Oehme, van Sweden Associates, landscape architects.

p. 70: (left) Brian Vanden Brink, photo © 2005; Design: Sally Weston, architect; (right) Photo © Tria Giovan.

p. 71: Brian Vanden Brink, photo © 2005.

p. 72: (left) Photo © J. Paul Moore; Design: The Porch Company; (right) Photo © Allan Mandell; Design: Duley Mahar.

p. 73: Photo © Allan Mandell; Design: Joyce Furman.

p. 74: (left) Brian Vanden Brink, photo © 2005; Design: Mark Hutker & Associates; (right) Brian Vanden Brink, photo © 2005.

p. 75: Photo © Allan Mandell

p. 76: (left) Photo © Deidra Walpole; Design: Kennedy Landscape Design Associates; (right) Photo © Deidra Walpole; Design: Ruby Begonia Fine Gardens.

p. 77: (top) Photo © Dency Kane; Design: Don Morris & Harry White; (bottom) Photo © Deidra Walpole; Design: Mayita Donos Garden Design.

p. 78: (top) Photo © www.kenricephoto.com; (bottom) Photo: © Deidra Walpole; Design: Ruby Begonia Fine Gardens.

p. 79: Photo © Mark Turner; Design: Patricia & Robert Lundquist.

p. 80: (top) Photo © Jerry Pavia; (bottom) Photo © Deidra Walpole.

p. 81: Photo © Mark Turner; Design: Larry & Stephanie Feeney.

p. 82: Photo by Todd Meier, © The Taunton Press, Inc.; Design: Alan Franz.

p. 83: (top) Photo by Steve Aitken, © The Taunton Press, Inc.; Design: Jim Scott; (bottom) Brian Vanden Brink, photo © 2005; Design: Horiuchi & Sollen Landscape Architects.

p. 84: (top) Photo © Mark Turner; Design: Larry & Stephanie Feeney; (bottom) Photo © J. Paul Moore; Design: The Porch Company.

p. 85: Photo © Mark Turner; Design: Terry Lehmann.

p. 86: (top) Photo © Mark Turner; (bottom) Photo © Allan Mandell; Design: Claire and Jamie Wright.

p. 87: Photo © Deidra Walpole; Design: Foxglove Design.

p. 88: Photo © Deidra Walpole; Design: Virginia Robinson.

p. 89: (top) Photo © Allan Mandell; Design: Robin Hopper and Judi Dyelle; (bottom) © Allan Mandell; Design: Joyce Furman.

p. 90: (left) Photo © Jerry Pavia; (right) Photo © Tria Giovan.

p. 91: Photo © Allan Mandell; Design: Ron Wagner & Nani Waddoups.

p. 92: Photo © Tim Street-Porter.

p. 93: (top) Photo © Tim Street-Porter; Design: Tom Beeton; (bottom) Photo © Tim Street-Porter; Design: Page Marchese Norman.

p. 94: Photo © Tim Street-Porter; Design: Nancy Goslee Power.

p. 95: (top) Photo © 2005 Carolyn L. Bates/carolynbates.com; (bottom) Photo © Tim Street-Porter; Design: Page Marchese Norman.

p. 96: (top) Photo © Lee Anne White; Design: Desert Sage Builders; (bottom left) Photo © Lee Anne White; Design: Michelle Derviss; (bottom right) Photo © Lee Anne White; Design: David Thorne.

p. 97: Photo © Deidra Walpole; Design: Mayita Donos Garden Design.

p. 98: (top) Photo © www.kenricephoto.com; (bottom) Photo © Deidra Walpole; Design: New Lead Landscape Design.

p. 99: Photo © Lee Anne White.

p. 100: (top) Photo © Dency Kane; Design: Cathy Cullen; (bottom) Photo © Deidra Walpole; Design: Green Scene Landscape Design.

p. 101: (top) Photo © J. Paul Moore; Design: The Porch

Credits *continued*

Company; (bottom) Photo © 2005 Carolyn L. Bates/carolynbates. com; Design: Catherine Clemens, Clemens and Associates, Inc.

p. 102: Photo © Jerry Pavia.

p. 103: (top) Photo © Jerry Pavia; (bottom left) Photo © Mark Turner; Design: Larry & Stephanie Feeney; (bottom right) Photo © 2005 Carolyn L. Bates/carolynbates.com; Design: Catherine Clemens, Clemens and Associates, Inc.

p. 104: (top) Photo © Deidra Walpole; Design: Green Scene Landscape Design; (bottom) Photo by Jennifer Brown, © The Taunton Press, Inc.; Design: Rosalind Reed.

p. 105: Photo © Tim Street-Porter; Design: Annie Kelly.

p. 106: Photo © Lee Anne White; Design: Konrad Gauder.

p. 107: (top) Photo © Deidra Walpole; Design: Kennedy Landscape Design Associates; (bottom left) Photo © Deidra Walpole; Design: Green Scene Landscape Design; (bottom right) Photo © Lee Anne White; Design: Desert Sage Builders.

p. 108: (top left) Photo © Lee Anne White; Design: Simmonds & Associates; (top right) Brian Vanden Brink, photo © 2005; Design: Horiuchi & Sollen Landscape Architects; (bottom) Photo © Deidra Walpole; Design: Green Scene Landscape Design.

p. 109: Photo © Lee Anne White; Design: Michelle Derviss.

p. 110: Photo © Lee Anne White; Design: Simmonds & Associates.

p. 111: (left) Photo © Lee Anne White; Design: Michelle Derviss; (right) Photo © Tria Giovan.

p. 112: (top right): Photo by Andy Engel, © The Taunton Press, Inc.; Design: Ron Cascio; (bottom right) Photo © Allan Mandell; Design: Jeffery Bale; (left) Photo © Lee Anne White.

p. 113: Photo by Andy Engel, © The Taunton Press, Inc.

CHAPTER 4

p. 114: Photo © Lee Anne White; Design: Joan Lewis, Cathy Feser, & Ruben Gonzales.

p. 115: Photo © Tim Street-Porter.

p. 116: Photo © Deidra Walpole.

p. 117: (left) Photo © Allan Mandell; Design: Des Kennedy; (right) Photo © Allan Mandell; Design: Joanne Fuller.

p. 118: Photo © Allan Mandell; Design: Ron Wagner and Nani Waddoups.

p. 119: (top left) Photo by Jennifer Benner, © The Taunton Press, Inc.; Design: Lucy Hardiman; (top right) Photo © Anne Gummerson Photography; Design: Nan Patternotte; (bottom) Photo © Deidra Walpole; Design: Hannah Carter.

p. 120: (left) Photo © Jerry Pavia; (right) Photo © Deidra Walpole.

p. 121: (top) Photo © Anne Gummerson Photography; Design: William Riggs; (bottom) Photo © Anne Gummerson Photography; Design: Sarah Schweizer, architect, and John Slater, landscape designer.

p. 122: (top) Photo © Deidra Walpole; Design: Hannah Carter; (bottom) Brian Vanden Brink, photo © 2005; Design: Robinson & Grisary, architects.

p. 123: (top) Photo © Tim Street-Porter; Design: Joseph Marek; (bottom) Photo by Steve Aitken, © The Taunton Press, Inc.; Design: Jim Scott.

p. 124: (left) Photo © Lee Anne White; Design: Jeni Webber; (right) Photo © Allan Mandell.

p. 125: (top) Photo © Allan Mandell; Design: Portland Japanese Garden; (bottom) Photo © Allan Mandell; Design: Michael Schultz.

p. 126: (top left) Photo © Lee Anne White; Design: Jeni Webber; (top right) Photo © Lee Anne White; Design: Richard McPherson; (bottom) Photo © Allan Mandell; Design: Berger Partnership.

p. 127: Brian Vanden Brink, photo © 2005; Design: John Morris, architect.

p. 128: (top) Photo © Alan & Linda Detrick; (bottom) Photo © Lee Anne White; Design: Joan Lewis, Cathy Feser, & Ruben Gonzales.

p. 129: (top left) Photo © Allan Mandell; Design: Linda Cochran; (right) Photo © Tria Giovan; (bottom) Photo © Dency Kane; Design: Martin Viette Nursery.

p. 130: (left) Photo © Alan & Linda Detrick; Design: Marlise Johnson; (top right) Photo © Alan & Linda Detrick; Design: Marshalwick Horticultural Society; (bottom) Photo © Deidra Walpole; Design: New Leaf Landscape Design.

p. 131: Photo © Anne Gummerson Photography; Design: Nan Patternotte.

p. 132: Photo © Allan Mandell; Design: Nancy Hammer.

p. 133: (left) Photo © Tria Giovan; (right) Photo © Lee Anne White.

p. 134: (top) Photo © Allan Mandell; Design: Barbara Blossom Ashmun; (bottom left) Photo © Lee Anne White; (bottom right) Photo © Mark Turner; Design: Christine Haulgren.

p. 135: Photo: Brian Vanden Brink, photo © 2005; Design: Weatherend Estate Furniture.

p. 136: (left) Photo © Allan Mandell; Design: Tom Hobbs; (top right) Photo © Allan Mandell; Design: Mike Snyder; (bottom) Photo © Tim Street-Porter.

p. 137: (left) Photo © Lee Anne White; Design: Michelle Derviss; (right) Photo © Tim Street-Porter.

p. 138: (top) Photo © Tria Giovan; (bottom) Photo © Allan Mandell; Design: Dotty & Jim Walters.

p. 139: (top left) Photo by Todd Meier, © The Taunton Press, Inc.; Design: James Woodel & Kimmy Tilley; (top right) Photo © Tim Street-Porter; (bottom) Brian Vanden Brink, photo © 2005; Design: Polhemus Savery DaSilva.

p. 140: (top) Photo © Dency Kane; Design: Richard Cohen & Jim Kutz; (bottom) Photo © Tim Street-Porter.

p. 141: (left) Photo © Allan Mandell; Design: Roger Raiche & David McCrory, Planet Horticulture; (right) Photo © Deidra Walpole.

p. 142: (top) Photo by Jennifer Brown, © The Taunton Press, Inc.; Design: Lucy